1-29-74

Hardcover: $7.00
Paperback: $3.00

CHRISTIAN FAITH IN BLACK AND WHITE: A PRIMER IN THEOLOGY FROM THE BLACK PERSPECTIVE. Religious and social ideas as seen by the Black community. Among the subjects considered: Why not just plain theology? savior and creator; the exodus; spirituals; violence; original sin; power; justice; love; individual vs corporate action; scandal of particularity; end justifies means? why Christ is Black; Jews and slavery; melting pot vs ethnic variety; African empires of the past; redemption; repentance; reconciliation; problem of evil; the Church; the last things.

THE AUTHOR: Warner R Traynham studied at Dartmouth College; Christ Church, Oxford; Virginia Theological Seminary. He has served as minister in Baltimore and Annapolis, Maryland; in Cambridge, Massachusetts, in the Chaplaincy to Harvard and Radcliffe students; and in Roxbury, Massachusetts, as rector of St Cyprian's Church.

At present he is Director of Black Studies at The Boston Theological Institute, a consortium of eight theological schools in the Boston area. He is also Instructor in Pastoral Theology at The Episcopal Theological School in Cambridge, Massachusetts.

CHRISTIAN FAITH
IN BLACK AND WHITE

A PRIMER IN THEOLOGY FROM THE
BLACK PERSPECTIVE

by

Warner R Traynham
Director of Black Studies, The Boston Theological Institute
Instructor in Pastoral Theology
The Episcopal Theological School, Cambridge, Massachusetts

A ⅃ ∫ ∞ ◇ ≡ | ∩ Ω
PARAMETER PRESS, INC
705 Main Street, Wakefield, Massachusetts 01880
United States

The quotations from the Bible are taken from the Revised Standard Version of the Bible, copyrighted 1946 and 1952 by the Division of Christian Education of the National Council of the Churches of Christ in the USA and used by permission.

Library of Congress Catalog Card Number 73-85538
International Standard Book Number
for hardcover edition 0-88203-004-3
for paperback edition 0-88203-003-5

Printed and bound in the United States of America by
The Murray Printing Company, Forge Village, Massachusetts 01828
and
Robert Burlen & Son, Inc, Bookbinders
Hingham, Massachusetts 02018

Composition by Jane L Keddy, Wakefield, Massachusetts 01880

CONTENTS

To

Jocelyn Phyllis

WHY NOT
JUST PLAIN THEOLOGY?

This book is about a phenomenon called *Black theology.* In its present form and under its present name, it is a new phenomenon. In the face of it, Christians of both races have asked, Why do we need Black theology—or white theology, for that matter? What is wrong with "just plain theology"—thinking about God in the way we have always thought about him? The question is a good one. It presupposes, however, that such a thing as plain theology is available. The first contention of Black theology is that plain theology is not available and never has been.

Plain theology is usually conceived to be the theology of the Bible, the theology expressed in the biblical record. Close examination of scripture, however, reveals many theological perspectives, not one. Some ideas in the Bible apparently represent a progression from simple to more sophisticated views; some simply represent different perspectives; some are apparently contradictory. In any case, the biblical material must be interpreted. The task of the theologian is to be an interpreter, to develop a consistent perspective which can correlate the biblical themes.

Thinking about God, or any other kind of thought, is done from a perspective— usually that of the thinker, although it is important to note that some individuals and groups have thought along lines laid down for them by others whose experiences and perspective were different. In such cases people think the thoughts of others rather than their own. Such theology is at heart inauthentic. It is false to the experience of those involved. Whatever perspective the original thinker

adopts is in large measure shaped by his experience although his gifts and insights enter in.

What has passed for plain theology has always been white theology: white theology from an English perspective or from a German perspective, etc, formed in the feudal period of medieval Europe or in the liberal period of the Enlightenment or in the more pessimistic period following the First World War.

If one understands that plain theology has never existed, then Black theology makes sense. It is Black people doing theology which is authentic for them. Black theology arises when Black theologians and thinkers reflect on the Christian faith from their experience in the same way that whites have been doing for centuries from theirs. Clearly the thinker brings his own imagination, his own creativity to the task.

Black theology is not limited to what Blacks have "always and everywhere believed and practiced." It has a teaching and a leading function. It should break new ground and take new initiatives, but the primary datum of a shared experience as Black people determines its character and shapes its reflection.

A similar kind of reflecting is going on now also in Latin America and elsewhere in the Third World. They too have discovered that the traditional theology does not take account of their experience and therefore often does not fit it. In fact, they have found, as many Blacks in America have, that too often there is an identity of interest between the prevailing theologies and the oppressor. Often these theologies sanctify the social system, or they stress patience for the oppressed.

The trials of the oppressed are interpreted as necessary for the good of the whole community or as keys to a salvation that will come by and by.

In American theological circles, Black theology has a double perspective. It brings to theological reflection the particular experiences of Black people, and, because that experience has been shaped in the vortex of oppression, it brings also the experience of the oppressed. Other liberation theologies bring other ethnic or social experiences, but they are all combined with the experience of oppression. This is what they have in common. This is their core.

Because, in action, race is a fundamental category of perception in American life and because the races of color are relegated to the end of the line and the bottom of the heap, here in America a theology of liberation takes a racial name. The term *Black theology* reflects, pinpoints, and dramatizes the perspective, its source, and its concerns. In order to symbolize the cause of liberation, it takes the name of those among the oppressed who, because of their numbers and their history, have the farthest to go toward liberation.

This book addresses itself to some of the issues raised when one does theology from this perspective.

A word to the Black reader: You are as aware as I that Blacks in America have a task, a destiny, like it or not. We generally agree on what that task is. It is called variously *achieving first-class citizenship, taking our place in American life, being free to do our own thing,* etc. You also know that our disagreements are concentrated in the area of tactics: How do we get from where we are to where we want to be? Black theology addresses the question of our task: What is God's purpose in this situation? What may we as Christians do toward achieving that purpose? While we have found direction and sustenance in the Christian faith over the centuries, it has always had to be reinterpreted so that we can understand our present life in the light of God's eternal purpose. From the days of slavery until the present, we have been dined on a gospel of accommodation and admonished to turn the other cheek in the face of injury.

But we have seldom taken the gospel as a whole and looked at it from our angle. Jesus was, after all, one of us in that he was oppressed as we are, despised and rejected as we have been. Black theology takes this fact seriously and boldly asserts that what we have been fed is white theology, a theology hopelessly accommodated to the oppressors' perspective. The intent of Black theology is to redress the balance, to correct the distortion: to declare what is gospel for the poor, the blind, the imprisoned, the despised.

This task is essential if the gospel is to be saved for a community grown tired of less than their due in a land of plenty. It is essential if that community is to hear and be saved by that gospel.

A word to the white reader: Most Black theologians claim at least to be writing for a Black constituency, and that is proper. Yet one of the peculiarities of the situation of the poor and the oppressed in America is that they are a minority, surrounded by whites. This is not only a reality which affects discussion, it will also affect the outcome of that discussion.

It is, therefore, appropriate to say to the white reader more than a "You may read this if you like." All conversation among Blacks is in some sense shadowed by whiteness if not about whites. The reverse is not true. This is one reality you must know. Rejection is not an occasional experience among Blacks; it operates even when we are not conscious of it. It operates in the fact that we live one place rather than another, work one place rather than another, etc.

Oppression and liberation may seem to you unnecessarily limiting categories for theology, appropriate perhaps for an ethnic group like Blacks or Latinos, but not generally. The contention of Black theology, however, is not that ethnics need their own theology but that no theology can be Christian if it is not shaped by these categories of oppression and liberation. It is not only a constructive task that we undertake for a few, but a critical task that is undertaken for all.

Read the gospel from the perspective of the oppressed, try to understand what they understand, hear with their ears if you can, and see if plain theology is not white theology. See if plain theology does not comfort the oppressor either by sanctification or silence.

Then see if you can make that act of identification, if your understanding of the "freedom with which Christ has made us free" does not begin to be deeper and more precise at the same time that it becomes more urgent. See if your appreciation of universal concerns is not corrected and sharpened by an understanding of these particular concerns. If this is not the case, reexamine again the role of the exodus and the offering of Jesus as real events in your understanding of life and faith.

Clearly in my lifetime, one of the most vital periods for the life of the church and the nation, if not the most vital, was the period known as the civil rights movement. Pro or contra, it animated our lives, stimulated our thoughts, provoked sacrifices and heroism. Like the gospel message, of course, it also brought fire and sword, setting father against son, mother against daughter, inspiring men and women and dividing them. That was

no accident. The nation did not simply briefly engage a great moral issue. It found itself briefly in the exhilarating and terrifying grip of the gospel itself. Black theology declares that this is no accident: that the force of the gospel surfaces here because this is what the gospel is about.

The fact that we speak of Black theology rather than civil rights theology indicates the discovery of dynamics and needs among Blacks which that movement spoke to but neither exhausted nor satisfied. But the reasons for Black rather than civil rights theology are in part what all our subsequent discussion will be about.

Finally a concluding word about this book. It is called a primer in theology. A primer is an introductory volume, which raises issues that you will face in more depth as you continue your study. It is intended to deal with some of the issues and to give you some background on them. No one writes an introduction to any subject without slanting that introduction and without making some constructive suggestions as well. This book is no exception. The field dubbed Black theology, or Black liberation theology, is in its present stage embryonic. So almost every volume that is written becomes part of the corpus to be criticized, utilized, or discarded as the field enlarges.

The primary function of this volume is to interpret rather than to resolve the issues, to set them before the reader as simply and precisely as possible. If the reader gains a better understanding of what is involved in this often misunderstood area, the author will consider his effort vindicated. If the reader's understanding of his faith is in any way enhanced and deepened, the author will consider that the result, not of his efforts, but of your openness and the grace of the

Holy Spirit who has animated the lives of Black people through three centuries.

Let me conclude by thanking all those who have encouraged me in this enterprise and especially, with an expression of appreciation, first to Dr Gayraud Wilmore, who supported me in the completion of this task and who kindly read the proofs and made numerous suggestions. Secondly, let me record the fact that without the initial suggestion, prodding, and expenditure of hours, days, and months in editing, correspondence, and advising of Mrs Jane Keddy this book would never have seen the light of day. She first described its possibilities and visualized them for the author. Her persistence, drive, and follow through are a cause of wonder.

These two individuals have been midwives at this birth. The heredity of the child, its features and foibles are mine, however, and I must answer for them.

Lastly, let me thank my wife Phyllis who has endured with patience and bright irony my many projects, all the while inspiring and encouraging me. To her this volume is dedicated.

W.R.T.
Roxbury, Massachusetts
August 1973

Chapter 1

SAVIOR AND CREATOR

Black theology is the understanding of the experiences of Black people in America in terms of the Christian gospel. Until very recently, Black theology was confined to sermons preached, prayers prayed, and songs sung in Black churches plus the style of life those churches adopted.

Recently, in the face of charges that Christianity is a white man's religion and the instrument of enslavement, those who profess to be Christians and are Black have been called to give a reason for the faith that is in them. They have been called to examine their faith in the light of their experience and that of the group to which they belong. That examination is not novel for Black Christians, but the ordered written presentation of it is.

In a time when one detects an aimlessness in both the white community at large and the white church in particular, it may be worth *their* while to attend to such explorations of the faith since it is in the nature of America that Black experience reveals as much about the life and destiny of the white majority as it does of the minority and since the proper understanding of the faith is an urgent concern for all Christians.

If we look at scripture, we find two themes appearing early in the Old Testament: (1) individual righteousness or obedience and (2) social justice.

Many people believe that the key event in the Old Testament is the event known as the exodus, where Moses is portrayed leading a group, later to become the Jews, out of Egypt, delivering them from slavery.

Israel is delivered from Egypt because the people are being oppressed there.

The exodus from Egypt is the normative event for the understanding of Jewish history. Everything which preceded it as well as what followed it is colored and interpreted in terms of it. For instance, in the book of Genesis we find the folk legends which tell of the prehistory of the Jews. When Israel looked back at this period, they read into it the call from God to Israel to become a special people and the promise of deliverance and land, which was actually realized in the exodus event, the giving of the law, and the entrance into the promised land.

In deliverance from slavery, in the conquest of a land, and in the subsequent organization of a nation—in these concrete events, the biblical understanding of what God is like were formed.

God had called them out of Egypt and promised to preserve them if they would be his people, a people whose peculiar destiny was to discover and then to show men what God was like and what he expected of men. These events shaped and determined all else that Israel was to discover about God and about its mission to be a "peculiar people."

No matter what your viewpoint, it is not natural to expect a nation of slaves to lay down their tools at the brickworks and walk off the job, go into another land, and establish their own kingdom. Even in an enlightened democracy, this is not something that would be expected, and Pharaoh's Egyptian Empire was not an enlightened democracy.

In the 26th chapter of Deuteronomy the heart of Israel's faith is expressed in the creed to be recited on the Feast of the First Fruits[Deut 26:5-9]:

> " 'A wandering Aramean was my father; and he went down into Egypt and sojourned there, few in number; and there he became a nation, great, mighty, and populous. And the Egyptians treated us harshly, and afflicted us, and laid upon us hard bondage. Then we cried to the Lord the God of our fathers, and the Lord heard our voice, saw our affliction, our toil, and our oppression; and the Lord brought us out of Egypt with a mighty hand and an outstretched arm, with great terror, with signs and wonders; and he brought us into this place and gave us this land, a land flowing with milk and honey. And behold, now I bring the first of the fruit of the ground, which thou, O Lord, has given me.' "

The idea of salvation or deliverance was at root and source a community idea. God had delivered the whole people from slavery. He had delivered the "populous nation" of Israel from bondage. He was their savior, therefore, and their deliverer.

All subsequent developments of the concept of savior and deliverer stem from the ways that the prophets of Israel interpreted the event of the exodus from Egypt. Moses is the prophet par excellence because he is the prophet of salvation. He interprets salvation.

Moses was the means by which Israel's salvation from Egypt was accomplished. Moses was also the herald of the God who made the idea become real, who put it into action.

In the ancient world, the reality of slavery was common and concrete. It was there for everyone to see. It was a prevalent and present fact. Israel did not have to imagine what it was like to be a slave. Slavery was at hand, to be examined, even centuries after Moses' time when Israel had long been delivered from the experience in Egypt.

Even though it was their deliverance from slavery that had been the determinative event that made the Hebrews a peculiar, chosen people, it is noteworthy that the Hebrews did not eschew the practice. The Jews held slaves. So did people in the rest of the ancient world, doubtless rationalizing the practice by the same economic and political ideas.

It is significant, however, that the Jews never seemed to be completely comfortable with that institution. Like countless peoples throughout history, they did not extend the full meaning of humanity to the people outside of their community. Nevertheless it is interesting in this connection to look at the Levitical proposals for the Year of Jubilee, which, alas, were never put into effect. In Leviticus 25 we read:

> The Lord said to Moses on Mount Sinai, "Say to the people of Israel, When you come into the land which I give you, the land shall keep a sabbath to the Lord. . . .
>
> "And you shall count seven weeks of years, seven times seven years, so that the time of the seven weeks of years shall be to you forty-nine years. . . . And you shall hallow the fiftieth year, and proclaim liberty throughout the land to all its inhabitants; it shall be a jubilee for you, when each of you shall return to his property and each of you shall return to his family. . . .
>
> "And if your brother becomes poor, and cannot maintain himself with you, you shall maintain him; as a stranger and a sojourner he shall live with you. Take no interest from him or increase, but fear your God; that your brother may live beside you. You shall not lend him your money at interest, nor give him your food for profit. I am the Lord your God, who brought you forth out of the land of Egypt to give you the land of Canaan, and to be your God.
>
> "And if your brother becomes poor beside you, and sells himself to you, you shall not make him serve as a slave: he shall be with you as a hired servant and as a sojourner. He shall serve with

you until the year of jubilee; then he shall go out from you, and his children with him, and go back to his own family, and return to the possession of his fathers. For they are my servants, whom I brought forth out of the land of Egypt; they shall not be sold as slaves. You shall not rule over him with harshness, but shall fear your God."

During this Year of Jubilee the bondsmen of Hebrew ancestry were to be freed. Israel's view of slavery was always influenced by their experience in Egypt.

Now let us leave Israel and return to the Black community in this country. It is evident that the Black slaves of America early discovered the inevitability of their deliverance from slavery and the source from which that deliverance would come.

The one record of ideas which has come down to us intact from that time is the music of this people, particularly the music that expresses their longing, their cries to the Lord their God for deliverance from affliction. This is the music that we know as the spirituals.

Commentators aplenty have, after examining the spirituals, pronounced them completely personal and otherworldly. I do not believe this is true of the spirituals, but how does it happen that it could be maintained that a faith founded in social deliverance and justice could yield a purely personal, otherworldly concern? Did Christianity work a transformation on the ancient Hebrew faith, or, more precisely, did Christianity continue and emphasize that transformation?

The faith founded on a divine act in history—the salvation of a community— gradually became universalized and spiritualized. What had been offered to Israel in an historical situation was offered to all men as a possibility for their personal and moral lives. Salvation was not only historical, having to do with communities and overt acts, it was transhistorical—relevant to personal and eternal values. It delivered men not only from sinful situations or the consequences of selfishness and injustice but from selfishness, from individual myopia, from sin itself.

As a result of this second focus upon personal salvation, upon each man's concern with his own psyche and his eternal destiny, many have concluded that the Church's interest is limited to such matters and is therefore wholly irrelevant to social change. All too often that assumption has been justified by our performance and our manifest interest.

But the Old Testament stands as an insuperable obstacle to the conception of Christianity as purely personal and otherworldly. Early in the Church's life a theologian named Marcian suggested that the Jewish Bible be dropped from the Christian scriptures. The Church fathers wisely rejected this first challenge to the integrity of our faith. The Old Testament, anchored as it is in the exodus story, certain as it is of the concrete acting of God in human history, reminds us of the roots of the Christian faith and is a necessary corrective for our tendency to spiritualize the New Testament. We need constantly to be reminded that, for those who wrote the New Testament, scripture was not what they wrote, but our Old Testament. They left much unsaid because it is said in the Old Testament. They would find very strange indeed our tendency to set the personal aspect of the faith in opposition to the social.

If then one lays aside, first, the prejudice for which the commentators on the spirituals are largely responsible and, secondly, the American historian's editing of history, especially as it concerns the Black man, then the spirituals are seen to reveal a profound understanding of the Christian faith in its personal, anti-sin dimensions, but also in the faith's meaning for community and history. Many spirituals are a cry for personal peace, for deliverance beyond the Jordan of death. But many are cries for an all too historical Moses and the crossing of a Jordan that is more like the Ohio, cries for freedom from the slavery of this world, rather than about the gulf between us and eternal rest.

I am convinced that most of the spirituals are coded to permit them to be sung and their message to be told while white people were present, because white people almost always were present.

Consider the abortive insurrections of Gabriel Prosser in 1800 or of Denmark Vesey in 1822 in which thousands of slaves were implicated or the famous uprising of Nat Turner in which sixty whites were killed in a single day. Consider the countless smaller revolts of slaves against the institution that enslaved them. Then one begins to realize that only a very dull reviewer could miss the meaning of such lyrics as

"Thus saith the Lord," bold Moses said,
    "Let my people go.
"If not, I'll strike your first-born dead,
    "Let my people go."
Go down, Moses, way down in Egypt's
    land.
Tell ole Pharaoh, "Let my people go."

Or

O Mary, don't you weep, don't you
    mourn,
O Mary, don't you weep, don't you
    mourn.
    Pharaoh's army got drownded.

Or

Didn't my Lord deliver Daniel?
He delivered Daniel from the lion's den,
Jonah from the belly of the whale,
And de Hebrew chillun from de firey
    furnace,
    And why not every man?

Even lyrics as bouyant and apparently frivolous as these:

L'il David play on your harp,
    Hallelu, Hallelu,
L'il David was a shepherd boy.
    He killed Goliath and shouted for joy.

are dangerous reminders that the faith of Christians is a faith of weakness aligned with right, triumphing over evil, though for the moment evil is stronger.

Bondage in the Egypt of America seemed without promise of redemption, but Black Israel survived, and it did so partly because the human creature clings tenaciously to life, however constricted. But Black Israel survived also partly because they hoped not only for eternal deliverance—they did hope for that—but for temporal and historical deliverance in this world, as well.

The underground railroad, the flight of slaves, the burning of property, the poisoning of masters, the records of malingering and self-mutilation, the revolts all belie the southern picture of a tranquil and satisfied Black population. In the light of these historical events, so do the spirituals.

The Black community saw itself as comparable to the Israel of old—Israel in Egypt. Also they saw their condition as comparable to that of their crucified Lord. Both Israel and the Black community were held in bondage. Both the Black community and Jesus suffered, and they suffered, they believed, for a purpose. The bondage theme and the deliverance theme were primarily connected with Israel. The suffering theme and the purposive emphasis were identified with Christ. Christ's suffering was necessary to save mankind. Israel's suffering made possible a just society. In Deuteronomy 10:18–19 there is a remarkable capsule statement of the social implications of Israel's experience. It is about strangers or foreigners, called "sojourners" here: The Lord your God "executes justice for the fatherless and the widow, and loves the sojourner, giving him food and clothing. Love the sojourner therefore; for you were sojourners in the land of Egypt."

In the mosaic law and in the comments that the prophets made about the event of the Jews' exodus from Egypt, we see many different concerns, but there is nevertheless one central theme: Israel is called by God to build a just society.

It is possible to find a summary of almost all the warnings of the prophets in the passage in which Amos says [Amos 6:4-6]:

> Woe to those who lie upon beds of
>   ivory . . .
> who sing idle songs to the sound of the
>   harp . . .
>   but are not grieved over the ruin of
>   Joseph!

Those who are themselves oppressors or who in any case are comfortable and undisturbed by oppression are condemned by the prophets and are called on by the prophets to right the wrongs that the prophets reveal.

Thus in Hebrew thought God is first encountered by man as being active in history—real reportable history, the kind that appears in the headlines, not just in the human-interest column. He is encountered as acting in a particular way, not as a God who is affirming the status quo, but as a God who is effecting change —change that costs somebody something, but change that, for the deprived, is cause for rejoicing and thanksgiving.

In particular, God acts by straightening out the relations among men, rectifying them, making the relations right.

Freedom and justice are the key ideas. Oppressors and the oppressed are the characters.

It is out of this setting that the Judaeo-Christian experience comes. It is to this that Jew and Christian must be true, and it is by this that claims to be part of the Judaeo-Christian experience must be judged.

It should be noted too that the first conflict in which man sees God acting is not between individuals, but among communities—not between individual wills, but within the structures of society.

The prophets of the Bible deal frequently with individual behavior, of course, but almost always it is the behavior of kings and their counselors, people whose individual judgments affect the shape of society and its structures.

I emphasize this point, that the Jewish people became aware of God in the conflict of social structures, in the relations existing in communities. It is necessary to be aware of this because the issue of justice is always a structural matter in society. Only secondarily is justice a matter for individuals.

Among the members of the church I frequently find a highly developed awareness of individual responsibility and an inclination to deal with the problems of race exclusively on the level of individuals. In a democracy where individual members of society have some power to affect structures or institutions, a structural question is, of course, also an individual matter. To deal profitably with the issue of race, however, it is important to remember that it is the structural aspect of race that is "the problem." The individual's response is important (at least to the oppressed) only as it leads men to change or resist changing the structure that is oppressing.

Let me clarify. Society is a collection of structures, or institutions. The dictionary defines a structure as a "complex system considered from the point of view of the whole rather than of any single part." The structure or system of segregation was a network of laws and customs designed to maintain the Black population as second-class citizens. It didn't matter if the restaurant owner was a good man or a bad one. If the law or the custom forbade Blacks to eat with whites in a restaurant, the owners would not let Blacks in—because society (the system, the structure) forbade it. Only when sufficient men of good will acted together to change the structure of segregation did that conscious system fall.

The problem was the structure. It took individuals acting together to change that structure. The personal morality of any of those individuals was irrelevant to the change. It was their public morality, their determination to right an objective public wrong that decided the outcome of the conflict.

Today the Black community is still at the bottom of the social and economic heap. It is there not because it is innately inferior or because it has no wish to rise. It is there because the system—the objective structures of society—work to keep it there.

It is irrelevant whether or not these structures were specifically designed for this end, as the system of segregation was. The result is the same. Let me give an example.

One state in the union gives an examination for bus drivers on which Blacks have consistently scored lower than whites. As a result, few Blacks drive buses. Persons are placed on a list in order of their test scores. Blacks down the list have been hired, and personnel men declare that they are as good bus drivers as men who rank far above them on the list.

Why? The test does not test driver's skills. It tests such skills as verbal aptitude and mathematics—things that are irrelevant to the job. More important, it is a culturally biased test. It was made up with a white constituency in mind.

Cultural exams have been held by the courts to be discriminatory.

The man who made up the test was probably not deliberately seeking to exclude Blacks. He just didn't think about them in connection with his test. The executive who decided to use this test, instead of one that would test necessary skills, probably merely wished to keep the tone of his company at a certain level. The people who administered and scored the exams may have been fine people genuinely dismayed by the discriminatory result. But the structure, the system, was discriminatory, and the good will of those who administered it was canceled out from the beginning.

Indeed, the continuation of such a system in the face of its results makes the original intentions irrelevant and those who presently administer it, guilty.

When the problem arises from someone who is biased, the problem is solved if the biased person is converted or removed. If the problem is the way things have always been done, the structure must be changed. This, of course, is not a new idea.

Doubtless many Egyptians got along well with the Hebrews and treated their Hebrew slaves well, like Pharaoh's daughter, who found the baby Moses hidden in the basket on the river. When she found him, "the babe was crying. She took pity on him and said, 'This is one of the Hebrew's children.' . . . And he became her son." Nevertheless, in spite of individual kindness, the question of slavery remained—a structural question having to do with the injustice of a system which allowed men to own other men.

The reality of oppression was not affected by declarations from the oppressor of his affection for the oppressed, however true they might be. Nor was the right to be delivered from oppression affected by the personal virtue or lack of it in the oppressed. According to the Bible, the Hebrews were delivered from oppression because they were in need of deliverance, not because they deserved it. The prophets spoke against the oppressor because the system of the oppressor was unjust to the oppressed. The prophets were for the oppressed because they were oppressed by an unjust social system, not because the oppressed were good.

One other point that is important to note here is that the prophets were speaking out against the Church—the Hebrews, God's chosen people—because they were oppressing their brothers and others, once they had become prosperous in the land of Canaan after their own deliverance from oppression in Egypt.

Some of you may be familiar with the illustration of the hungry man. If I come along and put a dollar in his hand, I have changed his prospects objectively. I may give him the dollar out of concern for him (the old-fashioned meaning of charity, which was like our word cherishing), or I may give him the dollar out of duty, or I may be trying to appear virtuous to others.

To God and me, and perhaps in the long run to the hungry man, the subjective reason for my action is important. In the meantime, however, my act has modified a social fact, regardless of my motivation. The man can eat, and, from his viewpoint, that is what is important.

The idea of a savior in the Judaeo-Christian tradition referred originally to one who altered a people's objective situation in history. Only afterward did it apply to God's concern for each individual's eternal destiny. In the same way, the idea of creator arose in the Judaeo-Christian tradition because the Jews first of all historically encountered God as a creator. He created a people from a motley collection of slaves and gave them a land and made them a nation. This very concrete reality is the source of these two very broad terms: savior and creator. This concrete reality of making a nation of a collection of slaves was certainly not lost on the Black population that produced the spirituals and who peopled churches both before and after the Civil War.

This was a reality that escaped the white population by and large, however.

When the slaves were first brought to this country, plantation masters resisted the first attempts of zealous clergy to make converts among them. The masters were afraid that Christianity would make the slaves dissatisfied. But no less a personage than the Bishop of London insisted that Christianity would make the African better slaves, not worse, that Christianity related to their souls and spiritual well being and would leave their bodies and their legal status unaffected.

The idea has been held by many people for centuries that the Christian religion has to do exclusively with the state of man's soul or with relations between individuals and personal acts of giving to those less fortunate than we are.

This strange idea is still alive.

Few Americans, the world's last individualists, will admit to understanding anything in terms of structures and social patterns. How much more difficult is it for them to comprehend other biblical insights like corporate responsibility. For example, at one point in the book of Jeremiah [31:29-30], the prophet says

In those days they shall no longer say:
"The fathers have eaten sour grapes,
    and the children's teeth are set on
    edge."
But every one shall die for his own sin;
each man
who eats sour grapes, his teeth shall be
    be set on edge.

In short, the group shall no longer be held guilty for the fault of a member, but each individual shall pay for his own faults. In terms of guilt, this unquestionably is a sounder principle, but in terms of the consequences of evil, the proverb is still perfectly true. The fathers *have* eaten sour grapes, and the children's teeth *are* set on edge.

Children do suffer for their fathers' faults.

Children do profit from their fathers' ill-gotten gain.

Children are left to solve problems that their fathers created.

Nowhere in contemporary American life is this proverb more evidently true than in the area of the relations between the races.

Finally, the way in which the Hebrews encountered their savior and creator was generalized by the Hebrew prophets to apply to all men. He was their savior and creator because he had delivered them, led them out of old lands and old situations, and made nations of them.

Thinking in terms of judgment, Amos reminds the chosen people that they are not unique in their encounter with God. Nor can they disregard God's call when they hear it. Thus Amos the prophet encourages others to understand their history in the way that Israel understood hers. God's saving is for all of us, and part of the way that God saves us is through judgment [Amos 9:7-10]:

"Are you not like the Ethiopians to me,
O people of Israel?" says the Lord.
"Did I not bring up Israel from the land
of Egypt,
and the Philistines from Caphtor and
the Syrians from Kir?
Behold the eyes of the Lord God are
upon the sinful kingdom,
and I will destroy it from the surface
of the ground;
except that I will not utterly destroy
the house of Jacob," says the Lord.
"For lo, I will command,
and shake the house of Israel among
all the nations

as one shakes with a sieve,
but no pebble shall fall upon the earth.
All the sinners of my people shall die by
the sword,
who say, 'Evil shall not overtake or
meet us.' "

In the fullness of time it pleased the savior to act in response to the cries of his Black children, and this nation's slaves were freed.

For a long time, almost a hundred years, the freeing of the slaves was talked of as a great national act, and the President, Lincoln, was called the Great Emancipator. Today, while the world celebrates the New Year on January 1 and the Church at large celebrates the Feast of the Circumcision, in Black churches, some of them, Emancipation Day is commemorated.

Lincoln is not praised, though he was unquestionably a great man and a profound one. Yet his action in freeing the slaves was dictated by the requirements of war. He was big enough to admit it. Had the war gone better for the North, emancipation would at best have been postponed. At worst, who knows?

The issue of slavery certainly was involved in the war. However, the nation is not praised for the emancipation. Though slavery was a question, the nation's mind was unsettled and, like Mr. Lincoln, more concerned for the preservation of the union and its political and economic goods than for the moral question of slavery.

No, on January 1, God is praised for his deliverance of his Black people.

One historian once commented that, before the emancipation of the slaves in the United States, no group of people that was oppressed by another people had ever received their freedom without any effort of their own. Insofar as that statement is true, like Israel, the Black community can profitably see in the emancipation the vindicating activity of God.

In the slave revolts, in the Black troops who fought for the Union and supplied it, and in the struggle for real freedom which has occupied the last 100 years, however, the reality has been underscored that God requires man to cooperate with him in bringing his goals to full fruit. By the same token, the lie is given to that historian's allegation that the Black community received its freedom without any effort of its own.

Chapter 2

THE SCANDAL
OF PARTICULARITY

One aspect of Christian theology has until recently received short shrift in systematic presentations of the faith. I refer to "the scandal of particularity." Usually in discussions of the incarnation, the formula runs, "God became man." That is scandalous enough, but it does not cover the ground.

In theology the word *God* is both a proper name and the name of a class. The one called God exhausts the class or the category; that is, there is only one God in the classification *God*. For instance, during the Middle Ages there was belief in a mythical beast called the unicorn, which had interesting properties. But there was only one unicorn, so it exhausted the class of creatures called by that name. Such a one is God.

On the other hand, *man* is the name of a class but not a proper name, for there are many men. In order for God to become man, he had to become not *man* but a particular man. In order to participate in the class or group called *man*, he had to become one of the men. He became a first-century Jew.

This is the scandal of particularity: He became a particular man in a particular situation. From this particular expression one may draw universal applications.

But one must take the particular expression seriously, and we as Christians have tended not to.

The scandal of particularity relates to the choice of Israel among the nations. You have heard the old saw,

How odd of God
To choose the Jews.

The argument of Black theology begins here with the insistence that the particulars of the divine action are not accidents, that God is fundamentally concerned with the relations between men and that the fundamental distortion of that relationship is the oppressor-oppressed relationship evident both in Israel's relationship to Egypt and in Jesus' relationship to men. This is why James Cone [1970] *, for instance, calls Jesus "the oppressed one." Only if we take seriously the particularly expression, the mundane, secular meaning of God's activity here on earth, the level at which he makes demands upon us that we can meet, can we then adequately appreciate their universal and their "spiritual" meaning.

The scandal of particularity lies in the fact that there is not a neat correlation between the absolute quality of God, whether it be conceived as love or justice or righteousness, and any particular human person or group or experience. Another way to put it is that God's activity is conceived as pure and unalloyed while all our acts result from mixed motives, all our virtues embrace some vice, etc.

Israel often wondered why she had been chosen rather than some other people. Some clearly concluded that they deserved it somehow. The prophets always insisted that it was an act of God's free choice. His will was not coerced by human deserts. Israel sinned. Jesus was tempted. There is no neat correlation between the perfection of God and any historical realities.

*In the bibliography, full information is given about works referred to in the text. The dates in brackets serve to distinguish among several publications by the same author.

On the other hand, the God who acts and finally becomes incarnate in history is no stranger to history or the world. He made it and presumably he approves this scandalous relationship. Therefore it must have meaning, meaning that has implications for us. In the New Testament there are two passages which illustrate what I mean and lead us into those implications. The first is Luke 6:20 and following. The second is Matthew 5:3 and following. They are both beatitudes. The second, Matthew's, is the better known passage and begins, "Blessed are the poor in spirit . . . , blessed are those who mourn . . . , blessed are the meek . . . , blessed are those who hunger and thirst for righteousness . . . , blessed are the merciful . . . , blessed are the pure in heart . . . ," etc. The emphasis here is on what we call "spiritual" virtues or values, qualities that cannot be immediately empirically tested. They are clearly virtues rather than conditions that are blessed.

But look at Luke's list. It is in two parts. First, "Blessed are you poor . . . , blessed are you that hunger now . . . , blessed are you that weep now . . . , blessed are you when men hate you. . . ." Then come the woes. "Woe to you that are rich . . . , woe to you that are full now . . . , woe to you that laugh now . . . , woe to you when all men speak well of you. . . ." This second set seems to judge people on their conditions, conditions that can be empirically and externally demonstrated.

We have between these two passages the same problem that whites and some Blacks feel about designating a theology as Black or equating white with oppressor or Black with the oppressed. The external evidence does not seem to jibe with the internal state. Some whites identify with the oppressed, some Blacks with the oppressor, just as you cannot equate the poor with the poor in spirit. I have a theory that different portions of scripture are useful to correct or comment on the particular problems or possibilities of different times in history. On that basis, I would say that today the Lukan beatitudes are more important than the Matthean, for what we need today is not to be convinced that God is concerned about "spiritual things," about inward qualities of life. Doubtless he is, and we do believe it. Rather, we need to be convinced that he is outraged by poverty more than by the sins of the poor, by men growing fat off the lives of others rather than by the faults of those others.

The particular is always ambiguous. It is not neat. As I have said, the prophets did not stand on the side of the poor and against the rich because the poor were virtuous but because they were poor, because they were victims and did not have an equal chance to be good or bad. It is the inferior-superior, rich-poor, better-worse relations that are a stench in the nostrils of God. What a man can do by way of virtue or vice is in some real measure determined by his circumstances or the group with which he is identified. If a poor man steals to feed his family, or even his ego, it is simply not the same as when a rich man embezzles so that he may become richer. The differences in their circumstances make it difficult to compare them fairly as two individuals.

The particular is always ambiguous, but God has chosen to express himself through it. Therefore its ambiguity cannot be an accident.

It may be said that all the fundamental doctrines of the Christian faith are anchored in particular and secular, worldly, facts. That is to say that God takes seriously particular people and particular conditions and our daily, worldly, secular life. It is also to say that universal principles and implications rest on very practical and precise facts and expectations. The Judaeo-Christian tradition was born in a context of oppression and the deliverance of a particular people at a particular time. That deliverance did not free them from the faults and foibles of humankind. It did not even deliver them from the temptation to themselves become oppressors. But in that deliverance God was identified as deliverer, and they were freed for other possibilities.

Whenever men experience deliverance, they experience God. Whenever men are liberated, God liberates them. Wherever men experience oppression, they experience the Anti-Christ, the Devil. Wherever men are oppressed, the Devil oppresses them. This is not necessarily a judgment on the motives of any individual man, although it may be. It is rather a judgment on an observable condition and its implications.

Until you have experienced concrete historical liberation, spiritual liberation will be an idea without moorings, a free-floating balloon. If you have experienced concrete liberation, you are more likely to know what spiritual liberation means and to know that they are not opposites but aspects of the same thing. If you are not concerned for the poor, what does it mean to say you are concerned for the poor in spirit? If you will not feed the hungry food which you have, how can you possibly know what to give to those who hunger and thirst for righteousness?

Of course it is unfair to say, "Blessed are the poor." Some poor people are rascals. Of course it is unfair to say, "Woe to you rich." Some rich people are philanthropists. Of course it is unfair to say that the only theology is Black theology. Some Blacks are oppressors. But between rich and poor, which would you be? Between Black and white,

all other things being equal in America, which would you be?

It was unfair to all other people for God to choose Israel and to all other men for God to choose Jesus. The particular is always in the historical sense unfair, but the universal is unhistorical and therefore in a sense unreal.

I mean, for instance, to say, "Blessed are the poor in spirit" is fine, but then one must ask, Was Martin Luther King, Jr, poor in spirit or Albert Schweitzer or Franklin Roosevelt, and so on. When the universal becomes real, it becomes particular, then we begin to disagree about who is who. But it is only on the level of the real that anything matters.

The particular is always unfair, but God's particulars are always much fairer than man's. If the poor sin, it may be penury that tempted them. If the rich sin, will they say it was because God blessed them? "They have their reward." The rich, the mighty, the great, the respected, the Ins as opposed to the Outs have what they have in order to share, so that those who have not may praise God and that they may know the joy of doing the will of God. But if the mighty ones use what they have for themselves, the others must call on God, and God must hear them in a way in which he will not hear the great and the mighty, for in that situation the great and the mighty are thieves and will flee from him.

There is abroad in the Black community a conviction that Christianity is a slave religion, a religion introduced by the white master to keep his slaves meek and tractable with a promise of better treatment in the next life. It is concluded that Islam or the traditional African religions are the only faiths appropriate to religious Blacks.

Christianity is, of course, a slave religion, though not quite in the sense its detractors mean. It is a religion which originated in slavery for and among the oppressed. The apostle Paul says [1 Cor 1:26] of the original Christians that "not many . . . were wise . . . , not many were powerful, not many were of noble birth." For not many such people care about the liberation of the poor and the discriminated against.

At this point let us take this opportunity to address a matter which in one way or another haunts any discussion of Black theology or liberation theology. We have in many ways and in various circumstances asserted that the gospel is liberation—that the thrust of the gospel is toward freeing people from objective and subjective oppression so that they may be fulfilled. So that they may realize abundant life.

The truth is that the Church has not always seen its mission in this fashion at all. Certainly the New Testament and the early church literature are full of references to combat with the devil and the objective powers of oppression. There is a lively understanding of the principalities and powers. The Book of Revelation, for instance, is in many respects a case of seditious literature of the most inflammatory kind, containing thinly veiled judgments on current oppressive structures as well as critiques of those of the past. But there is another strain in this literature also. The strain that concentrates on perfection. This is best represented by the concern expressed, when taken out of context, in the Epistle of James [1:27] to "keep oneself unspotted from the world"—the concern for the few ransomed out from the lost. These two strands exist and frequently intertwine. They are not equal in weight or strength,

however, and it is the contention of Black theology that the strain of liberation is determinative and far outweighs that strain known to religious history as sanctification. Certainly, at the source of revelation, in the New Testament and the early Church period, liberation predominated. What is true, and for our purposes essential to understand, is that, with the gradual acceptance of Christianity as the religion of the Empire, and then of all Europe, several things changed.

The numbers in the Church grew, and at some point in the 4th century an oppressed minority found itself a tolerated group and then largely in charge. With that, the emphasis shifted. Having suddenly so many great within its ranks, the Church was embarrassed at its words about the great, so it tended to read them to refer to the puffed up. Its words to the poor largely became words to the poor in spirit, which incidentally a rich man could be. It shifted emphasis from the particular to the universal and from the deliverance of the oppressed, sick, hurting people to the deliverance of all men from sin and eternal death, never mind their secular circumstances, their conditions in regular life. Musically, we say the Church had both options but shifted largely from her major to her minor key. The shift was subtle but real. Both themes continued, but the churchly concern for sanctification increasingly predominated.

The Church was able to do this because the world had changed, or rather appeared to have changed. The images of warfare with the princes, the real princes of this world, the oppressive powers, etc, seemed inappropriate. Instead of the Body of Christ in a hostile world, or the People of God on pilgrimage, or the Army of Divine Liberation, the Church was seen primarily as an ark—Noah's Ark, and her motto was, *Extra ecclesia nulla salus*, outside the Church there is no salvation. The emphasis was not on arming for the conflict but on preservation of the truth and then on right belief. During the Dark Ages when order in Europe had largely deteriorated, the Church was an ark, the central locus of order, consistency, and sanity in a hard, rapacious world.

But with the coming of what historians call the medieval synthesis, the Church and the world appeared to merge. Christ had conquered, man was free—as free as God had meant him to be on earth. There was no enemy out there to combat except the Jews, who were themselves oppressed by the new order, or the distant Saracen, against whom Holy Crusades were mounted to liberate—not men—but the holy places. The Kingdom had come. The emphasis of the Church further shifted from liberation to sanctification, from freeing men for abundant life to perfecting men for eternal life. She became increasingly concerned with the perfection of souls and the means of grace to aid them on their way. The armor of Christ gave way to the means of grace. From being an equipment and training center, the Church became a school for saints, an ecology lab trying to keep every individual's life "spiritually balanced" so that they would grow up into the fullness of the stature of Christ.

The focus was otherworldly because it was believed that the Church had won its conflict with oppressive powers here on earth. In actuality, it had simply joined them. It had shaped and now it sanctioned the status quo. To challenge any aspect of the social order was to challenge the faith. The levels of society were not seen as oppressive but as God ordained for the stability of society, and society was to be kept stable and orderly by the prince, the state, so that the Church could do its work of sanctification—so that the gospel might be truly preached and the sacraments truly administered. The world was one—no longer Church and World,

liberators and oppressors—but one world under the Church's authority and care. For administrative purposes, Christendom was cut in two. The emperor ruled the secular man, the Church the spiritual man. As the spiritual was the higher, so the Church's rule was superior, and the state wielded its sword always in the Church's defense. There were disagreements periodically about what was spiritual and what secular, but the disagreements were usually resolved. In any case, there was no disagreement about the principle. This arrangement endured until very recently as a matter of fact. While it endured, the Church was the State on its knees, and, between Church and State, they covered all the world that mattered.

During this period, sanctification was understood to be the key to the Christian religion. Jesus' arts of healing, liberation, etc, were seen not as revolutionary, but merely as acts of charity. They were fitted into the prevailing system. Even as late as the reformation, this view of the Church persisted. The major reformers— Calvin, Luther, Swingli, Cranmer—were not asserting the primacy of liberation over sanctification. They were arguing about the *true* preaching of the gospel and about the *true* administration of the sacraments. They challenged the way the Church was ordered, not the world view it purveyed. They were medieval men. Like many revolutionaries, however, they almost inadvertently ushered in ideas that would inevitably bring down this world view. The division of the world into the spiritual and the temporal (secular) with the Pope heading one and the emperor at least titular head of the other—this order, which baptized the prevailing social structure, held Europe in its grip a thousand years. During that time, men were taught more to be serviced by the

Church and to serve it, and less to serve God in the world. The world had already been vanquished.

With the reformation, it became gradually evident that the "world" could not so easily be tamed. The revolts of the peasantry during this time were regarded as unchristian because they rejected the established order, thus stirring up civil strife and making the task of sanctification more difficult. But the peasants perceived the so-called God given order as oppressive and found in scripture the promise of liberation. The forces unleashed could not be muffled, and the synthesis fell apart. Unfortunately, it takes a long time to break habits that have been centuries in the making. Long after the appropriate context has vanished, the Church still conceives of itself as an ark. Large segments still react as if the only thing needful is sanctification and the Church's only goal, eternal peace and the beatific vision. Christians are often offended at being asked to arm themselves for battle instead of simply subscribing to the means of grace and personal moral effort because for a thousand years they were told that this was the Christian's business.

So brief a synopsis of so much time is bound to be distorting, but the essential points hold. We have the need to reassert the liberation theme of the gospel because for so long our concern for sanctification overshadowed it and, while the two themes complement each other, that of liberation is fundamental.

The world changed long ago. The medieval synthesis fell apart 500 years ago or longer, yet we have not yet retooled. We continue to deny the change that has occurred or attempt to reestablish the old order. Puritan New England is nothing if not such an effort at reestablishment.

Instead of regaining its original concern for the oppressed and returning to its roots, the Church kept on acting as if nothing had happened. The means of grace continued to be offered to a world crying for liberation. Universal answers continued to be given to particular questions, and men concluded that Christianity was an opiate, a slave religion, a thing designed by oppressors to maintain them in power, and the treasure of the Church was forgotten except by a few, here and there, who read the old books with new eyes and encountered a different Christ, who served a different God. Like the prophets of old, they began to call Israel again to her roots.

Black theology belongs in this category of radical theology (radical = pertaining to the roots). It calls the Church to consider its particular origins and what they mean for its life. It calls her to consider her corporate nature and concerns before she runs off to individual and universal concerns lest she falsify the latter by misunderstanding the former.

The sacred-secular dichotomy is an instance of this misunderstanding, the separation of life into sacred and secular parts. When we do this, we imitate the medieval synthesis, without the subordination of the secular to the religious, and the synthesis flies apart. We abandon the particular for the universal; we equate the universal with the "spiritual" and therefore the particular with the "secular," which allows religious men to deny any connection between religion and politics or any connection between morality and business practices, etc. One cannot reflect upon the experiences and the needs and the hopes of Black people in America without discovering that the distinction between the sacred and the secular can serve only the slave master, never the slave, which is to say that it serves the cause of oppression, however expressed. Those who have plenty are thus rendered immune from criticism from the Judaeo-Christian tradition, even while they claim to subscribe to it.

It is a situation which would have amazed the prophets.

For the Black man, much of his religious hope is for a change in secular circumstances, and a God interested only in sacred things is worse than useless. Such a God is a criminal. He is an enemy.

The ethical element in Black theology is large. It is large because ethics deals with behavior, and the attempt to distinguish religious behavior from secular behavior is more obviously bankrupt than the attempt to distinguish spiritual concerns from secular concerns. The ethical element is large because the question for Black theology is not, "Is there a God?" but, "Who is God?"

Ordinarily one might say that all theology presupposes God and sets about the task of asking who he is. Yet it has been my experience that whites tend to ask primarily the philosophical question, "Is there a God?" They seek proofs, reasons, etc. Blacks tend to be, for better or worse, more Hebraic. They ask, "Who is he?" "What does his existence mean for me?" "What does he say about my condition?"

When a white person says he does not go to church, his reasons usually circle around a denial of God's existence.

When a Black person laughs at church attendance, he usually says, "The church is a racket. God can't do anything for me." God's existence or nonexistence is not the issue. His effectiveness is.

One can oversell the point, but it is worth making. Black people have been in need of a God, a God who could affect their circumstances here and hereafter.

The white community has as a group been less aware of that need. The oppressor is seldom aware of his need for deliverance from the desire to dominate and to feel superior, which are the universal or "spiritual" faces of the particular instance of oppression. So long as he can escape being called an oppressor before God, he will never deal with these universal or spiritual forces. In theological terms the "white man's burden," so revered in the 19th and 20th centuries, is a mammoth rationalization for sin. It is a magnificent vice, as St Augustine said of the virtues of the pagans.

You see this emphasis on particularity, far from landing the Church in a quagmire of detail, has clear universal implications. The problem with the Church has never been that it was concerned with universal realities but that it ignored their relationship to particular circumstances and therefore distorted them.

Christianity is, after all, not a system of thought but a movement, not a school for saints but an army. Its concern for liberation from sin and death derives from its head-on involvement with those foes' practical expressions in oppression, sickness, and hurt. It is that encounter with particular evil that led to the further concern with universal sin and death. C S Lewis, the Anglican theologian, once observed that the difference between the present and the early Christian periods is that, for the early period, Christianity could be preached as good news because the men of that time knew they were locked in the grip of the powers of sin and death and needed deliverance, while contemporary man must first hear the bad news before he can hear the gospel.

It sounds like condemnation, and it is. It is encountered as wrath, and it is, but it is for modern man's own good. It is the left hand of love, what Martin Luther called the *opus alienus*, the strange work of God.

But it is not so strange to the Jews who lived during the holocaust of nazism. It is not so strange to the Blacks of America or South Africa or to the peasants of Latin America. To them, the left hand of love is the power of God for salvation, the only salvation that matters. To preach God to a hungry man and refuse to feed him is blasphemy. Luther called it God's strange work because he belonged to those who oppressed, who identified with law and order, for instance, against the oppressed who rose in the peasants' revolt to claim their rightful stature in the society of Reformation Germany. It must always seem strange to the oppressor. The question is whether or not he is able to recognize it as the work of God.

In this connection one finds in Black theology an emphasis on the corporate almost to the exclusion of the individual. This is the case because in human experience it is groups that are oppressed. Individual oppression is a specific instance of that group oppression. Israel, the poor, are groups. They are specific, ambiguous, and the objects of oppressors. Christ was oppressed because he identified with the poor, the publicans, the sinners of the land, with outcast groups.

In reality, of course, the oppression of a group is the sum or aggregate of the suffering of its individual members. Oppression is first an individual experience. Since that experience is common to many individuals, it pushes them together to compare and reflect upon their status and to share support and resources in the face of a common foe. The Black community is, at least in part, the creation of oppression. It exists in part because the oppressor conceives of it as a group and treats it as such. Black religion recognizes the individual nature of Black suffering and puts it in context.

From the perspective of the oppressor, however, the oppressed are not seen as people, let alone individuals. They are always dehumanized in order that they can be oppressed. They are referred to as "the problem." They are the invisible men. Because it is groups that are oppressed, it is groups that are liberated. It is a kind of demonic reversal of the corporate nature of mankind. Oppression is the fracturing of human brotherhood, not into individual parts but into groups which then lord it over one another.

So Black theology takes seriously the group life of humanity. It knows that men are capable of things as groups that they could or would not do as individuals and that a theology which considers man only as an individual is not a theology of liberation. Such a theology has ignored half the human experience and by so doing has distorted the other half. So the oppressors operate in groups and identify the oppressed as groups. An interesting aspect of the latter was, for instance, the laws that at one time or another appeared on the books of most of the states of this Union, defining what a Black person was by blood. They varied from place to place, and yet some definition of the group was necessary in order for it to be consistently oppressed.

This emphasis on the corporate quality of human life is intended to balance the individualistic, atomistic approach characteristic of western thought. But it is intended to point out that, because individuals are seen as members of groups, their being and behavior are affected by that identification. What may be appropriate for a person to do, all other things being equal, may not be appropriate for one who is oppressed or vice versa.

To tell the oppressor to turn the other cheek is one thing. To tell the oppressed to do this is quite another. To tell a free individual, if such exists, is still another. The situations are different, and they affect the meaning of the ethical and the theological. The particular circumstances alter the application of what we call universal concerns. The problem of violence, which we will treat later, is a very different question when applied to different groups. How different is, of course, the question.

At the heart of Black theology is this scandal of particularity, taking seriously the circumstances of revelation. The implications, as one might expect, are many, and we have just begun to discover them.

Chapter 3

SIN AND POWER

We have dealt with the concept of savior and creator. We considered how Judaeo-Christian man first got his ideas of savior and creator and what these ideas mean for racial relations in this country.

We found that both the idea of savior and the idea of creator grew out of a particular historical event, the exodus, when Israel was saved from slavery and created a people. Israel had been saved from her oppressor, and a free nation had been created out of the oppressed. In this experience of oppressor and oppressed, Israel first met God, for Israel knew that she had not saved herself from Egypt and that no other man had saved Israel from oppression in Egypt.

In the second chapter, we have looked at the implications of this particular experience as it affects the Church's understanding of itself and its God.

We see the relationship of the particular to the universal and the necessity of understanding the one to rightly understand the other. We have briefly reviewed the false distinction between the sacred and the secular, and finally we have noted that salvation is first corporate and only secondly individual.

Israel's prophets in later years saw the condition of oppressor and oppressed arise when Israel had settled down and become rich in the promised Land of Canaan, what we call Palestine or, roughly, the present country of Israel. Later in Israel's own life, when some of the Hebrews became oppressors and some were oppressed, the prophets saw this and on God's behalf challenged the Israelites who were oppressors, just as Moses had challenged Pharaoh.

The idea of justice in society is basic, therefore, in the tradition of the Jews and the Christians. The idea of justice among men comes before the Judaeo-Christian concern for individual goodness, and justice is the source of that goodness.

Let us now turn to another Judaeo-Christian viewpoint—that of original sin. This teaching holds that man's true character has been twisted and distorted.

This distortion in man's character stems from a lack of faith in God. Faith is, after all, reliance upon the trustworthiness of God to support us and to do well by us. Faith is trust in God, openness to his world and what he is doing in it. It is the willingness to align ourselves with him and participate in his liberating work. The opposite of faith is not doubt, but fear.

In the context of Black theology, the opposite of faith is the flight from liberation. For the oppressor, the opposite of faith is to rely on the support of the system of oppression. For the oppressed, the opposite of faith is the acceptance of oppression rather than risking revolt.

The result of fear is the search for something else to rely upon. This fear, this lack of faith, causes the twisting of man's actions and perspective because it is contrary to the way he was made, namely, to trust God. The result is the distorted world of original sin. As a result of faithlessness, man always, and ofter without knowing it, looks out for number one—because he fears that nobody else will look out for him. That orientation toward self is original sin. It is not an action, but a state of mind—a set of mind from which actions proceed.

Original sin is the inborn selfishness that colors our every thought and act unless we are redeemed, brought back by the savior to a relationship of trust. This distortion of man's real character by original sin is what makes social justice so necessary. Justice in this context is, first of all, the placing of individuals and groups on equal footing so that they can equally defend themselves. If one has an unfair advantage over another, it is very likely that the one on top will make use of his advantage. Let us take a look at some illustrations of original sin.

A husband and wife both notice that their apartment is becoming increasingly shabby. What to do? One of them goes and buys furniture. If it is the husband, he is very likely to buy living room furniture. That is the room in which he entertains his friends. If it is the wife who buys the furniture, she is likely to buy kitchen furniture if the kitchen is where she spends much of her time. Their actions are the result of their interests.

Unless love or thoughtfulness or caution enter in so that they sit down and discuss their needs, each one's interests and actions will be to his own advantage.

This self-interest is characteristic of the operation of groups as well as of individual persons. An illustration is the racism in the Church—the racism built into the structure of the Church as seen in the light of the teaching of original sin.

I am a member of the Episcopal Church's delegation to COCU, the Consultation on Church Union. This is a group of people who are discussing and planning ways in which Christian churches may become one [John 17:21-22]. The church bodies taking part in COCU are

The United Presbyterian Church USA
The United Methodist Church
The United Church of Christ
The Christian Church (Disciples of
   Christ)
The Episcopal Church
The African Methodist Episcopal Church
The Presbyterian Church in the US
The Christian Methodist Episcopal
   Church
The African Methodist Episcopal Zion
   Church

At the meeting in 1969, Bishop Jordan of the African Methodist Episcopal Church addressed the delegates. In his speech he made this observation: Before the three all-Black churches joined the consultation, there were no Black delegates at all for the three years that COCU had met, although there were sizable Black minorities in the member churches. When Black churches joined, delegation chairmen from the other churches had to look at their delegations to see how representative those delegations were.

Now all of the six other churches have either a Black member in their delegation or among their seminarian observers. Bishop Jordan asked: If the Black churches stay and are absorbed into the church body resulting from the consultation, who will then ensure that the voiceless have a voice?

Or again, in the mass media: Until a few years ago you could watch TV and never know that there was a Black man in this country, unless you watched the news. You are not likely to make that mistake today, yet there are proportionally no more Blacks in this country now than there were then. It had to be pointed out that Blacks were not adequately represented and then hammered home.

Many of you will recall the story of David and Bathsheba. David sees and desires the wife of Uriah, one of his soldiers. He takes the man's wife, and, when she becomes pregnant, he finds it necessary to eliminate Uriah and take Bathsheba into his harem and legitimitize his child. It is arranged for Uriah to be killed, but the matter does not escape the attention of the Lord, who sends his prophet Nathan to the King [2 Samuel 12:1–9]:

> He came to him, and said to him, "There were two men in a certain city, the one rich and the other poor. The rich man had very many flocks and herds; but the poor man had nothing but one little ewe lamb, which he had bought. And he brought it up, and it grew up with him and his children; it used to eat of his morsel, and drink from his cup, and lie in his bosom, and it was like a daughter to him.
> "Now there came a traveler to the rich man, and he was unwilling to take one of his own flock or herd to prepare for the wayfarer who had come to him, but he took the poor man's lamb, and prepared it for the man who had come to him."
> Then David's anger was greatly kindled against the man; and he said to Nathan, "As the Lord lives, the man who has done this deserves to die; and he shall restore the lamb fourfold, because he did this thing, and because he had no pity."
> Nathan said to David, "You are the man. Thus says the Lord, the God of Israel, 'I anointed you king over Israel, and I delivered you out of the hand of Saul; and I gave you your master's house, and your master's wives into your bosom, and gave you the house of Israel and of Judah; and if this were too little, I would add to you as much more. Why have you despised the word of the Lord to do what is evil in his sight? You have smitten Uriah the Hittite with the sword, and have taken his wife to be your wife. . . .' "

We who are most clear on the faults of others are often very dull about recognizing our own.

Original sin is not something that belongs only to the white man. It is part of the Black man's experience and character too. Many Blacks tend to see white as evil, just because it is white, and vice versa.

Christianity gives us freedom from a falsehood like this. In this country there is a difference in the results of actions by Blacks and by whites, however. This difference arises from their different histories. When Blacks act out their own self-concern, for the most part they affect only themselves. When whites act out their self-concern, because they are in power like David, too often they affect Blacks more directly than they affect themselves. This is the source of the injustice. Structural injustice is a possibility only for those in power.

The Old Testament prophets understood this very well. They moved among the great because evil in high places is more evil since it affects more people. The great should be better than the small because they can do more damage, not, as is often thought, the reverse.

Not only does original sin affect what we do, but, most important, it affects how we think about our deeds. T S Eliot once said that it is hard for those who live near a bank to doubt the security of their money.

It is hard for those who have profited from a system to believe that it has victimized others. It is hard because they have no first-hand experience of being victimized by the system. We are ourselves, not someone else. If we are the profiteers, we cannot really appreciate what it means to be the victim. It is hard to believe that our profitable system is unjust because to believe that will either make us feel guilty or make us wish to rock the boat, which is dangerous.

In human society, change toward justice comes usually only from the dissatisfied or from those who identify with them. Now the view that the dissatisfied or the oppressed have of society is different from the view of the satisfied, and their timetable for change is different also.

The phrase *law and order* to a suburbanite means the safety of person and property, people continuing to have what they now have. To an inner city dweller, law and order is more likely to mean suppression and the unwillingness of government to deal with causes, preferring rather to deal merely with effects. It means continuing to be deprived.

Urban renewal to the wealthy and powerful means making the city suitable for habitation again. For poor and Black people, urban renewal means being uprooted from their homes, losing all they have built up for their families, whatever that may be.

The fear that the white community has of destruction and violence and its unwillingness to deal with the causes of these acts mean to the poor that the powerful have a greater concern for property than for people. The issue lies in who implements these programs and how, not in the ideas themselves.

Ghetto dwellers desire law and order. They desire safe streets, but they desire equality in the application of the law and real, not just apparent, order. The poor know better than anybody the need for urban renewal. They are the ones who suffer from urban decay. But they want renewal that includes them, not removal of the slum to another quarter in order that officials and businessmen can make money and young white exurbanites can live in safety closer to their jobs.

The story of the good Samaritan reveals the divine bias on these issues. The priest and the Levite pass by on the other side of the road from the wounded man. No doubt they had good and orderly reasons for passing by the wounded man: Probably one reason was the fear of becoming ceremonially unclean according to Jewish law and thus being temporarily barred from taking part in the divine service if the wounded man should turn out to be dead.

The divine bias—the viewpoint of God— is shown by this story of Jesus. It is the act of responding to real need that is held up for the follower of Christ to imitate. From whatever quarter the need comes, it is the response to need that is good, not first of all the maintenance of order or rules. The priest and the Levite are condemned while the hated Samaritan is praised because he responded to need.

On one reading, the condemnation of the priest and the Levite is unfair. They had, doubtless, good reasons to pass by. But the reality is that they did not meet the need of another human being. The judgment was perfectly fair.

Lord Acton's famous saying is based on the doctrine of original sin: "Power corrupts; absolute power corrupts absolutely."

It corrupts not only the action but also the vision of that action. I am of the opinion that, if the Black community had been cast by history in the role that the white community is in, the Black community could conceivably have acted in a similar way. Obviously it is impossible to second-guess history.

The point is that the role of oppressor is not inherent in whiteness. It is historically conditioned. Racism comes from sin, a persistent selfishness, rather than from the color of the skin or from one's ancestry. In any case, and this is the important point, history worked the other way.

Black theology has been criticized for emphasizing corporate sin to the virtual exclusion of individual sin. There are,

I believe, at least two reasons for this where it has been the case.

First, individual sin has received considerable treatment but not in the context of corporate realities. Little has been said in the Church about how corporate considerations—group considerations—change ethical situations. As a matter of fact, we could all agree that, all other things being equal, murder is wrong. But having agreed to that can we on that basis, or must we on that basis, condemn Nat Turner's rising in Southampton, Virginia, in which 60 whites of slave-holding families were killed in an attempt by the oppressed to throw off the absolute legal control of the oppressor? Under most circumstances we would agree that theft was wrong, but was it wrong to steal from your master who exacted labor without pay at the point of a gun or the threat of physical harm or extinction? We could probably agree that lying was wrong, especially if it hurt another person, but can it be argued that under the conditions of slavery the servant owed his master the truth? Is it not easily conceivable that his identification with his oppressed fellows demanded that, as a Christian, he should in many situations rather lie to his master?

These illustrations are all drawn from a clearly defined system, that of slavery. The argument of Black theology, however, is that, for too many in the Black community circumstantially and for all the Black community psychologically, there has not been sufficient change in 100 years to significantly alter this relationship between the races. On this assumption, the illustrations are in no sense academic. Concern with the ethics of group behavior and the relationship between positions in society and moral behavior, while arguable, are not irrelevant in any sense, yet these factors have often been ignored by theologians.

Secondly, the emphasis on liberation in Black theology has quite explicit implications for individual morality as well as for group action. The thrust is toward liberating activity, rather than the elaboration of a moral casuistry or a set of rules, which is why the subject often appears to be ignored. If liberation is the key to the gospel, then certain actions on both the individual and corporate level follow. Perhaps Black theologians would do well to spell these out as they relate to interpersonal relationships, but the implications are certain.

Chapter 4

POWER AND VIOLENCE

Let us turn now and consider violence in the light of our ideas about original sin. We cannot consider all sides of the question of violence, but we can deal with some of its meanings.

Webster's *New Collegiate Dictionary* defines violence as "an exertion of physical force so as to injure or abuse." It also defines it as "injury by or as if by distortion, infringement, or profanation." In short, violence is doing injury to the integrity of a person, a relationship, or a thing.

There are, then, at least two types of violence: the noisy type, which we normally think of, that involves physical force; and the quiet type, where injury is done by distortion or infringement of rights or by profaning the sacred, not primarily through the use of physical force.

When those in power do violence, usually they prefer to use the second method. When men protest violently or when they express fear violently, they usually chose the former.

We in this country, as has been observed more than once, have a history of physical violence. Soon after the War of Independence, the federal government, on purpose or by chance, entered upon the violent extermination of the American Indian. For generations that race was on the verge of extinction.

There was the violence inevitable in any slave system where one man possesses the power of life and death over another. In the relations between the races, this violence continued after slavery. the 1920s saw race riots begun by whites against Blacks in the great cities of the north. These riots took a larger toll in both loss of life and property than have

any race riots since. Between emancipation and the present, more than 3,000 Blacks have been lynched in north and south.

With the exception of the War of Independence, all this violence can be traced to the willful exercise of power or the grip of fear.

Compare this with the physical violence of the Black community. It begins with the revolts of the slaves against a system which enslaved them. It includes the reality of crime, the most prevalent violence loose in this community. It is self-destructive: murder, assault, arson, vandalism—the violence of the poor against the poor. Like most violence that is hit or miss, it speaks of the distress of the community and the frustration that for many have no legitimate expression, no real way to be told that will guarantee a hearing.

Then there were the riots of a few years ago in the ghetto where property was burned or stolen and persons killed. Race riots initiated by the majority race tell us something about society. They tell of the majority's fear of those they have oppressed lest the oppressed should escape and challenge the oppressor. They tell too of the majority's contempt, in that they may indulge in violence with impunity.

When the minority riots, that too tells us something about society. When a man destroys another man's property, usually he doesn't have any of his own that he can lose—either he has very little or what he has is well protected. In the case of riots in the Black community, the latter is certainly not the case. If the rioter had anything to lose, the doctrine of original sin would lead us to expect that, instead of being in the street, he would be home protecting what was his. Therefore, clearly the rioter can contemplate losing without trouble whatever he possesses. These riots then put a question to us.

How does it happen that in the richest nation in the world so many people believe that they have nothing to lose?

Many people ask about this violence as if it were a tactic. Yet this violence is not planned. It is not designed to achieve goals or to help the "cause." It is the eruption of hurt too grievous to be borne. It is the assertion of manhood in the face of its violation. To ask what effect such violence has on the liberation of the Black community may be useful. But to ask if it is wise, as if the Black community could prevent it, is like asking if it is wise for the top to blow off the tea kettle.

In terms of some goals, the answer may be no. But the relevant response to the event is to learn from it and get busy and turn off the fire. The riots of recent years are instances of men telling other men that they have had enough.

Enough of what? Enough of violence.

One of the great dangers of being in power is the temptation to be violent and call it something else. The establishment, whoever and wherever it is, has usually (though, as we have noted, not exclusively) preferred the quiet violence we spoke of, injury by or as if by distortion, infringement, or profanation.

For instance, in order for this Christian country to face the institution of slavery, Christian sensibilities had to be catered to. In other places and times, slaves were people integrated into the system of law with responsibilities and rights before the law. We, however, were unable to consider enslaving men, so we invented a

novel fiction: contrary to all appearances and previous experiences, these Negroes were not men. Subhuman creatures, cursed by God, supposedly with the curse of Ham, they could be treated as property pure and simple, like any other livestock.

The violence that was done by slavery to the psyches of men so regarded and so designated by law was far greater than any violence done to their bodies. That psychological violence worked by slavery has not stopped. It proceeded through the era of the Klan, through segregation in the north and the south, to the present ghettoization.

This point may be illustrated by the treatment of the Black Panther Party by the police departments of a number of major cities. The Panthers were outspoken in proclaiming the view held by much of the Black community regarding the police. It is no wonder that the police found the Panthers threatening. Even a quick examination of the facts shows, however, that, while most of the talk has been on the Panther end, most of the action was on the police end. The Panthers stockpiled guns but, by and large, they used the guns only in self-defense. On the other hand, many of the Panthers have been killed, and several were forced out of the country.

Less publicized but more insidious and more general is the violence evident in governmental disinterest in the drug scene so long as it was limited to the ghetto or in the issue of speedy justice, which for years has penalized the poor, a disproportionate number of whom are Black.

All kinds of things can be done or left undone in the name of law and order.

Recall the story of Ahab, Jezebel, and Naboth's vineyard. Naboth had a vineyard beside King Ahab's palace. Ahab wanted it, but Naboth, because it had been in his family for generations and he considered the land a sacred trust, refused to sell. Ahab brooded over that vineyard, and Jezebel, his wife, saw no reason why her husband shouldn't have it, even if it didn't belong to him and its legal owner refused to sell [1 Kings 21:8-19]:

> So she wrote letters in Ahab's name and sealed them with his seal, and she sent the letters to the elders and the nobles who dwelt with Naboth in his city. And she wrote in the letters, "Proclaim a fast, and set Naboth on high among the people; and set two base fellows opposite him, and let them bring a charge against him, saying, 'You have cursed God and the king.' Then take him out, and stone him to death."
> And the men of his city, the elders and the nobles who dwelt in his city, did as Jezebel had sent word to them. ... Then they sent to Jezebel, saying, "Naboth has been stoned; he is dead." ...
> Then the word of the Lord came to Elijah the Tishbite, saying, "Arise, go down to meet Ahab king of Israel, who is in Samaria; behold he is in the vineyard of Naboth, where he has gone to take possession. And you shall say to him, 'Thus says the Lord, "Have you killed, and also taken possession?"' "

Ahab wanted the vineyard. Naboth wouldn't give it up. So Jezebel stepped in and had Naboth duly and legally accused and executed for blasphemy and treason. Legal violence is not new, and it is available only to those who are in power.

It is significant that this particular story ends with the violent deaths of both Ahab and Jezebel.

History lives more in the hearts of the oppressed because much of what they possess are historical grievances.

Physical violence, violence to pride and self-image, the insult of being disregarded —all of this is not merely the heritage of the past. If it were so, one could say that the Black community is morbid. It is not morbid. This violence of former days is remembered because the Black community still suffers it.

Moreover, the violence inflicted is not merely the violence of individuals acting out their own personal prejudice. Some of that will always be with us.

The real violence comes from the structures of society.

When we have a Supreme Court judgment for desegregated education that has been in existence for 19 years, when the President of the United States stands with those who are avoiding the law and thus prolonging inferior and segregated education, when this is the condition in the land, why should the Black community develop confidence in law and order?

In the face of manifest chaos, calls for law and order have a certain reasonableness. In the face of the demand for justice and change, they ring very hollow indeed.

What is violence? Stealing five bottles of whiskey from an insured whiskey store that has overcharged for years? Or failing to pass an anti-rat bill in Congress?

What is violence? Refusing to pay a landlord until he plasters the falling ceiling? Or refusing to fix a ceiling because you know the housing market is tight enough so that someone will have to move into the slummy house?

What is violence? Striking a man because he uses his power to oppress you? Or striking a man because you know he cannot hit back?

What is violence? What is sin?

In this connection let us turn to one of the persistent issues in the dialogue among Black theologians and between them and the white community. The issue of violence can arise in a slightly different context. Black theology raises the issue of violence as a moral tactic for the oppressed in the struggle for liberation. The discussion circles around the phrase which James Cone [1969, 1970] popularized in his two seminal volumes in this field. Cone stated that the oppressed had the right to use "any means necessary" in order to cast off the chains of oppression. This phrase is significant for several reasons.

First, those who object to it usually interpret it to advocate violence, and they object by asserting that violence will lead only to annihilation—you can't win; or that violence will make impossible the ultimate reconciliation—integration; or that violence may be necessary but never Christian.

The phrase "any means necessary" is an ambiguous one. It implies that Cone at least is not prepared to eliminate any means to his end. That is to say, he is not prepared to advocate fighting a battle with one hand tied behind his back, especially when the other guy suffers no similar restraint and has a hundred pounds on him. The phrase does not propose a flight into wild, thoughtless violence, nor is it a proposal for cold-blooded guerilla warfare or assassination, options that many oppressed people have taken.

"Any means necessary" must be presumed to mean just what it says: any means the oppressed deem appropriate or called for by circumstances. The oppressed must determine the means and the necessity because the foot is on their neck. Only they can say when it seems that the throat will be crushed shut or the blood vessels ruptured or the backbone snapped. Nobody else cares enough to examine the body.

Certainly it comes ill from the one whose foot is felt to advise on the seriousness of the matter. The assertion that the oppressed only may make this moral judgment troubles many, but the oppressed are in the situation. They did not design it. Those who protest designed it, or at least they profit from it. Their exclusion from judgment, therefore, should

be a small price to pay for continuing to receive the benefits of oppression. In any case it is inevitable. Equally inevitable, of course, will be their judgment that the situation does not warrant whatever resistance is proposed.

Czarist Russia was outraged by the revolutionaries. Bourbon France saw no reason for the republican uprising. No oppressor has ever been able to see the morality of any revolution, except perhaps the one that placed them in power.

To bring the matter closer to home, for many years the NAACP was criticized and in some places outlawed as being an organization of agitators, racists, provocateurs, etc. The Klan rode against them. Before that, of course, it rode against uppity niggers who wanted to vote, keep the property they owned, sit anywhere on trains, etc. The NAACP, it was said, would ruin race relations and make racial harmony impossible in the future. After the climax in 1954, the NAACP was looking a lot better to whites compared with the bus boycott in Montgomery, where the fight was taken out of the hands of Negro intellectuals and white liberals and given to the common people. Martin Luther King, Jr, then became the villain. But the boycotts which forced men to change and threatened to disrupt race relations were not as bad to the ultra conservatives as the freedom riders. At least the boycotters were local people. And they refrained from activity. The freedom riders were outsiders, troublemakers, commies, demanding change by doing something, by initiating activity. Then came the sit-ins, which challenged America's most cherished principle, the unrestrained use of private property. After escalation, the cry went up, "This is too much. This will polarize the nation. It will be war."

Each cry was like old King Canute, who is supposed to have set his throne below the high-water mark and commanded the sea to stop rising. All he got for his trouble, of course, was wet feet.

Then came the cry for Black power and the abandonment of integration as a tactic and a goal. Would-be Cassandras were heard again as dire predictions arose in every quarter. Now Martin Luther King, Jr, who was once unbearable, seems to most as gracious a prophet as ever trod earth. Those who cursed him cast longing glances at his memory when they encounter churchmen who speak of using any means necessary for the liberation of the oppressed.

The oppressor is terrified by each escalation of method in the struggle because he does not believe in the struggle. It strikes, after all, at him. He is terrified and warns against every escalation of the struggle because he knows what he deserves and is afraid the oppressed will find out and give it to him. His estimate of the seriousness of the issue must serve his need to survive. That is why his estimate is so questionable. That is why his judgment may not be allowed to determine anything. And, because he has always held that no means is necessary, it is necessary to preclude no means, for so far he has adjusted to every tactic and to every approach.

Only when those identified with the oppressor identify with the oppressed, and establish their credentials as ones who identify with the oppressed, can their response be accepted as an advocacy of right rather than as oppressive self-interest. Whites tend to be stampeded by phrases, perhaps because they know what they would do in a similar case. The fact is that, along with advocates of radical militancy, the Black community has within it advocates of restraint, whose credentials are established for the Black community. No useful contribution is made by whites who desire to speak on the issue of violence without being identified with efforts to aleviate the causes for radical action—just the reverse. They increase the numbers of those opposed to them who might be impressed by their advice if their performance or lack of it did not so clearly show where they really stand.

Joseph Fletcher, formerly of The Episcopal Theological School in Cambridge, Massachusetts, in his several books and articles has persuasively asserted that, contrary to usual ethical theory, the end does justify the means. What else, he says, could justify it? Such a thesis raises the question, What is the end?

In the case of oppression, the end, of course, is liberation. One aspect of Black theology asserts that the end is sufficiently great to justify using any means necessary. Clearly not all ends will justify any means or, rather, any means necessary. It is asserted that this end will. Liberation or the expression of manhood in the quest for liberation is the end. The question Black theology puts is: "Is this not an end of such magnitude that, if the oppressed fail to grasp it by whatever means is necessary, they betray not only themselves but their creator?"

If this is not such an end, what is?

Others have raised the question of the appropriateness of some means, particularly violent means, to our ends. For them the end is conceived of not as liberation but as reconciliation. Without prejudicing the later discussion of reconciliation, the difficulty with this position must be considered. Deotis Roberts [1971], of Howard University School of Religion and author of *Liberation and Reconciliation,* is one proponent of this view from within the arena of Black theology. For him Black theology is not a theology of liberation, but one of liberation and reconciliation. For him reconciliation, like liberation, is historical and is largely equatable with the goal of integration. If whites and Blacks are to live together in America, then some things are not tactically useful, however morally acceptable they may be. Violence on the part of Blacks, especially planned and purposive violence, will render the goal, he believes, impossible.

The problems with this view are at least twofold. First, are we, either the Black community or the white, prepared to accept integration as the ultimate solution to the race problem in America? Only a few years ago certainly the vocal Blacks did. Whether the masses ever did remains a question. Certainly for many integration remains a goal, but just as certainly it is a goal that does not begin to have the motive power it once possessed.

Part of the disaffection with integration as a goal, of course, stems from the fact that the white community has never subscribed to it to anything like the extent that Blacks did. Further, considering the continued resistance on issues such as school integration, housing patterns, etc, there is no evidence that the white perspective has appreciably changed or that we may anticipate any appreciable change in the near future.

Part of the disaffection among Blacks stems from the perception that the goal of integration-amalgamation requires yet another cost to the Black community, the elimination of its integrity in exchange for acceptance. I mean by that that the inevitable corollary of integration was integration into a white thing. Integration is the logical extension of the great melting-pot theory of American society,

a theory which when actualized is designed to produce a White Anglo-Saxon Protestant nation. The nation's view of itself is that of a homogeneous whole, or rather that is its goal. Blacks have been consistently excluded because they do not fit that vision. They make the vanilla mixture mocha, at the very least.

Only recently has the merit of this theory been questioned. Only recently has the reality of pluralism in America been conceived of as a value and opportunity rather than as a problem to be homogenized away. But pluralism is attractive in a way that integration never was to those who believe that their racial and historical experiences have contributed values as well as disvalues to the recipients and to society at large. The question, "What does it mean to be an Afro-American?" means more to many Blacks today, intellectually or socially if not visually, than does the question, "How do I identify with the majority and pass?" The answer to the question is for pluralism, rather than integration, for group integrity rather than dissolution. Integration into the structures of society remains a goal. Integration into the white race socially or actually by and large has a declining list of adherents.

But if we consider integration into the structures of society as a share of the power and presence, will not violence erect an unscalable wall separating us from that goal? Whether or not violence proves to be, or is deemed, necessary, a cursory view of history should disabuse us of most of our misapprehensions along these lines, at least.

We referred above to the overt and covert violence practiced by whites upon Blacks in this land for longer than the republic itself has endured. Did that violence, protracted over 350 years, make communication between the races impossible? Perhaps it should have. In fact it did not. It is not violence but the duration of violence, not harm but the obtuseness of our society to the cries of the injured which have forced us to look elsewhere and to discover our ends in goals that do not wait on the white man's cooperation for realization. But the objection, of course, related to the white man's response to violence, not the Black's.

Here too history is illuminating. It is a sad fact that the endurance of violence by and large, and I have not forgotten the limited experience of Dr King's nonviolent moral crusade, has generated contempt and more violence, while violence, in the long run, seems to have had the reverse effect.

It is a general observation, elevated almost into a principle, that Americans are consistently more generous to their enemies than to their friends. It seems such a consistent reality that comic movies have been made about it. Especially is this the case when the nation has fought those enemies. Certainly the evidence of the Civil War is relevant here. The nation not only survived the war, but it may be said in many ways to have profited from the war. Despite the bitterness of the event and its traces, there obtains a mutual respect and a level of social intercourse which is far better than that which obtained before that conflict. In short, considering the oppressor's natural preachments about escalation and his performance in the face of escalation and considering the wider arena of history, experience fairly well belies the logical idea that violence will make the wounds impossible of healing.

Further, if the goal is otherwise conceived, the objection carries no weight at all. That is to say, if the goal is not integration, then the point of the objection is much less forceful.

Finally, there is the objection of which Major Jones [1971], of Gammon Theological Seminary and author of *Black*

Awareness, is the primary exponent in Black theology and for which, of course, there are many spokesmen outside the Black community. This objection is that violence is never moral. Jones wishes to combine a traditional Christian abhorrence of violence with an appreciation of the difficulty of the plight of Blacks in America. He is thus in the position of saying that, while violence may be necessary, it is in no sense theologically justifiable. But certainly either violence cannot be necessary then, or it must be theologically justifiable. If the two, necessity and justifiability, can be in the conflict that he sees, then God is not the Lord of history. His theology, if not his God, clearly is too small.

If a thing can be necessary, it must be good in that situation. In a larger, more normal context it may be evil, but in a constricted, abnormal context it may be good. A choice between two evils, when that is the only possible choice and a choice must be made, is a choice in fact between good and evil, and the lesser evil is the good.

After all, good and evil do not exist in and of themselves, but in relationship and in particular situations. Jesus, we are told, took whips to the moneychangers. He destroyed their tables and raised whelts on their backsides. He was also responsible for cracked shins, heads, skinned knees, or whatever else those men sustained in trying to escape his wrath. Either we must convict Christ of sin, or we must abandon the principle that violence is always contrary to love. Frederick Robertson, the English preacher, commenting on a Good Friday address on the repentant thief, once observed that scripture recorded one deathbed repentance, so to speak, so that no man need despair, but only one so that no man dare presume. The argument over the morality of violence, like that for deathbed repentance, cannot find much scriptural evidence in the New Testament (the Old Testament abounds in it), but, even in the life of Christ, there is too much violence to permit Christians to elevate nonviolence into an absolute maxim.

Violence as a means has its problems.

Perhaps it is using the weapons of the enemy. Perhaps for any given individual nonviolence is a viable alternative and moral lifestyle. Perhaps any individual can take upon himself the ultimate end of that stand, which is, of course, to permit himself to be killed without offering violent resistance.

But can he justify raising no violent hand to strike down the attacker of another? If he can justify it, is he at that point in any fashion morally superior to the man whose theology will permit him to strike that attacker down and to justify that act?

For many years, the Church, following a superficial interpretation of the injunction of the apostle James, tried to hold itself "pure and unspotted from the world."

It was no less a personage than St Augustine, however, who presented a justification for the adandonment of that stance and for involvement in the structures of the world. Essentially he said that we believe that Christianity is true and the pagans are in error. Therefore our judgment in worldly matters should be better than theirs because our understanding of the world is better. Therefore, while we would rather not be judges or magistrates at all, if there must be judges and magistrates, it is better to have Christians than pagans. That perspective has gotten the Church into a great deal of trouble, but it has at least gotten us into the world. While there is much wrong with the Augustinian formula, he rightly perceived that our task was to deal with the real world, not a monastic ideal, and he rightly perceived that God was the God of ambiguity as he

was of clarity and that God's good and evil frequently appeared as better and worse, but they were no less real and no less his own.

Three final observations about the issue of violence in Black-white relations and in Black theology:

First, the issue put sharply in the phrase "any means necessary" raises in a particularly effective way the seriousness of the situation and the moral determination that it shall be altered. What is being said is that the cause of liberation is the gospel cause and that it will be realized and that the oppressed and those who identify with them have a responsibility to join in effecting that end, whatever the price. It may appear a threat to whites. It is a challenge certainly to Blacks to join in the divine activity without counting the cost because it is his cause and not simply their own. At this point I think Major Jones' observation is valid when he notes that we are on God's side, not he on ours. We know he is Black because he has made us Black.*

Secondly, this issue, as all issues in this area of Black-white relations, is complicated by the fact that the Black community lives in the midst of whites, surrounded by whites, so that violence has always a witnessing aspect as well as a tactical one. Violence by a minority is a response which would undoubtedly bring quick overwhelming retaliation. It has been observed that the slave revolts were much less numerous in the antebellum South than in Latin America because whites always outnumbered Blacks here, and all the revolts that occurred were frustrated. The slave had before him no models of successful revolt. That slaves did continue to revolt is then a witness to the

*For a fuller discussion of the Black Christ, see Chapter 8.

determination of the human spirit to realize at whatever cost the divine promise of freedom.

To be in the midst of whites means, by the very nature of the case, that we seek a different kind of revolution from what men usually mean by revolution. We seek what Robert Frost called "half a revolution," not one where the Ins become the Outs and the Outs become the Ins but a revolution where the man who was on the bottom stands eye to eye with the man who kept him there. Violence then can never be aimed at the destruction of the white man, though it may be aimed at the destruction of some whites. Rather, it is aimed at getting him off our backs, as are all other tactics that may be used. The liberation of Black America cannot require the destruction of others except as they resist all other means to gain liberation.

Integrity requires that a man be who he is. The cost of that is finally determined by the man who resists the effort, not the man who seeks to stand.

Thirdly, the revolution so often spoken of in this context is in fact a very conservative revolution. Many have commented on the patience of the Black community in prosecuting it. Our tendency has been to exhaust one mode of operation before abandoning it and moving on to another.

The rate of escalation and the degree depend upon the resistance. The oppressed determine what is necessary to achieve their goal, but the oppressors, by their action or lack of it determine what is required. It is the rock which determines the force needed to dislodge it. Its mover merely tries until he finds out what that force is. The task, therefore, of constructive theologians is less to debate the moral or the tactical value of violence and more to interpret the divine outrage that a situation should be designed in which this violence could be deemed necessary for the liberation of this people.

Chapter 5

LOVE AND JUSTICE

Several times we have had occasion to refer to the tendency of Americans to see the "race problem" as an ethical issue between individuals. Christians are likely to move from this analysis—that personal prejudice or hatred is the problem—to the assertion that Christian love is the answer to that problem. In this context, they speak of racism and reverse racism, prejudice of white against Black and of Black against white, etc. The matter is seen as a kind of equality of hatred to be resolved with an equal expression of love on both sides. Just as the problem is seen to be primarily personal, so the solution is similarly seen. Christian love is conceived of as turning the other cheek, overlooking faults, being kind to persons, and other such attitudes.

We have already dealt with the whole issue of systems as opposed to individual actions, what we have at times called "corporate" behavior. We observed that systems, or structures, really determine interrelations between social groups and therefore between individuals as well. Just as the analysis of the situation as personal was inadequate, so the understanding of Christian love as simple kindness or forgiveness is inadequate.

Plato, in one of his dialogues, defines love as "the desire for the everlasting possession of the beautiful and the good." Using his definition, we might start by defining Christian love as "willing that every man everlastingly possess and be possessed by the beautiful and the good."

Given such an operating definition, we note first of all that Christian love is not "the desire," something that is involuntary, but "the willing," something that is voluntary. It is something located first in the moral will, rather than in the emotions. Many theologians have made this observation and this distinction. Filial love, love of family, is based on familiarity, comfort with familiar things. You know the old saying, "We love our children because they are our own." The love of family or friends is largely an extension of the love of ourselves. We perceive them as part of ourselves, by blood or by similarity of perspective. It is an affection which is so natural that it is expected. If members of a family do not feel this affection, we refer to them as unnatural. Love of family is socially conditioned and largely involuntary. It is not something you undertake to act out.

Erotic love is based almost entirely on an involuntary desire, a feeling. It is, of course, conditioned by our experiences, some of which we have no control over, some of which we have. The involuntary aspect of this love is indicated by the phrase "falling in love."

There are other ways of subdividing human uses of the word *love*, but this should suffice to make the point.

Christian love is not in the first instance a feeling at all. It may become a feeling because frequently acting a certain way develops in us the appropriate emotional affect. But to begin with, we have little control over the way we feel about any individual or group. Those feelings are socially conditioned. We do, however, have control over what we will. A brief perusal of scripture will show that Christian love is commanded. Love of family is commanded also, but closer examination shows that what is in fact enjoined there is a certain line of action, namely respect.

Christian love includes respect. One may say it is an elaboration of respect. It can be commanded because is is an act of will first, though later it may have feeling aspects. It is to will the fulfillment of the other, pure and simple. Plato's "desire for the everlasting possession of the beautiful and the good" has the same intent. Such possession was for him the fulfillment of human nature.

When Jesus healed men, those healings were acts of love, not affection. Love. He helped people toward fulfillment by restoring sight, or speech, or the power to walk. He fulfilled the promise of physical sense or power. When he healed the demoniacs, those were objective acts of love for he fulfilled the promise of mental health, etc.

To will that every man's potential should be realized and to initiate or support action to this end is Christian love. The motive of Christian love is response to the offering of Christ which he undertook so that each of us might have what he called "abundant life."

Christian love, then, is first of all a voluntary act. It has nothing to do with feeling or emotion in the first instance, but is motivated by a response to God's care and Christ's sacrifice for each of us.

Now if we try to apply Christian love to the relations of the oppressed and the oppressor, we discover that the implications differ for each group because a radical inequality exists. Oppression is the very opposite of Christian love. Oppression cripples, blinds, possesses in order to control. Oppression is the use of people as means entirely. Oppression and the oppressor restrict the realization of the potential of some men for special purposes of their own.

Oppressors can have affection or desire toward the oppressed but they cannot have Christian love.

The oppressed, on the other hand, find that their position requires that they find means to limit the power of the oppressor as the only possible expression of Christian love. If they do not, then they do not will the oppressor's fulfillment because they cooperate in his distortion. To deny men fulfillment, to deliberately frustrate them, is to twist and distort your own potential. The relation of master and slave or oppressed and oppressor falsifies the lives of both. The relationship asserts that one has the right to power and control to which he has no right and that the other does not have the right to power and control to which he does have a right. It is like being on a seesaw with someone of unequal weight. The game will work only if there is some equalization of the relationship. Otherwise one is too high and the other too low, and the game comes to a halt.

Christian love between people of unequal status requires as its primary goal the equalization of that status. If Christian love exists between individuals of the oppressor and oppressed classes, it can do so only in the context of revolution. That means that a white man in America can show Christian love to a Black, in the first instance, only by identifying with that Black and undertaking, as far as is in his power, to disestablish the oppressor and restore the God-given relationship between men and groups. This means that a Black man can show Christian love to a white man in the first instance only by asserting his integrity as an individual and the integrity of his group to the end of disestablishing the the oppressor and equalizing the relationship between them.

In the context of oppression, Christian love cannot be anything else but revolutionary. Furthermore, in that context, any relationship of love, whether it be desire or affection, that leaves the context unaffected is a sick love, a distorted love, an unChristian love.

When southern whites talk about the affection obtaining between themselves and "our nigras," insofar as they refer to any real relationship, they refer to a sick relationship—a relationship which makes one party more than a man and the other less, distorting each's view of himself and the other. It is sick because it is built upon a lie. It is unChristian because the devil is the father of lies. When the northern liberal declares his concern for the Black man but will not live next door to him or be vice-president in an organization where a Black is president or, on the other hand, approves uncritically everything the Black man says while according fellow whites a critical evaluation, that concern is a sick relationship, and when it is reciprocated it perpetuates a lie.

In a relationship between unequals, the first demand of Christian love is the equalization of that relationship. Affection and desire are focused on the self. They desire the possession of their object as it is. That is the only change they require in the relationship—possession. Christian love is focused on the other first and therefore must be concerned for the condition of that other. This is why affection and desire yield rewards, but Christian love must pay a price.

Christ died because those he threatened realized, even better than those he represented, that he was a revolutionary. They got his message that the great were not to tyrannize over the weak but, rather, enable them to stand. They perceived that he wanted to equalize men—to set them at eye level with their "authorities," and they killed him for it.

When we say Jesus was a revolutionary, we do not mean that he went about in fatigues. We mean the judges of Israel and Rome were right. He was a threat to their authority, not because authority is evil. It is essential, but because he denied a fundamental tenet on which their particular authority rested, namely, that some men, because of virtue or culture or race or color or whatever, are better than other men and have claims on those that they do not have to reciprocate.

For Jesus, authority was the child of responsibility, not of privilege; every man was a son of God, no more, no less. That was revolutionary then, and it is revolutionary now. For, since Cain killed Abel, men have exalted themselves over other men and claimed rights that are nowhere testified to in the universe. In short, they have built kingdoms on lies, and lies destroy those who believe them, those who suffer under them, and those who tell them.

If Jesus was a revolutionary and Christian love means the overturning of false relationships, what sense can we make of Jesus' ethic: "turn the other cheek; if a man requires you to go with him one mile, go with him two; blessed are you when men persecute you and revile you for my sake and the gospel's"? What can all this mean in this context of revolution? This question is consistently urged against any theology which takes seriously the revolutionary quality of the gospel and its commitment to actual, empirical change.

First, a word about Jesus himself. We have already discussed the implications of particularity. It has universal implications, but it has also specific limitations. Jesus' action was appropriate to his calling and his goal. Consider for a moment his circumstances. He had no boss, no time-clock to punch. He had no wife and children to depend upon him for support. He exercised no authority over men in the institutions of society. I mean he was not an employer, a judge, a policeman, etc. He apparently abandoned his trade and lived on the offerings of others who did work to earn a living. In the end he had to commend his mother to the care of a friend who presumably, unlike him, had a home in which to lay his head. He was what we call a "free spirit" in every sense. He moved through life unencumbered. We have no record of his ever having been sick. He died in his thirties and so suffered none of the inabilities of old age or the adjustment to declining powers. By the same token it should be noted that, while his life excluded many problems common to man, it excluded much of the comfort that enables us to bear those problems—comforts such as security, love of family, expectation of posterity, etc.

Jesus' life was particular, designed for a particular calling. That calling was to make men aware of the freedom which they possessed while oppressed so that they could address the causes of their oppression. His calling was to endure the cost of setting himself against the powers that oppressed so that men could believe that God was willing to endure all and able to triumph and make them triumph, too. Jesus' calling was: (1) to make men know that they had liberty of action even when being driven; (2) to make men know God was on the side of the oppressed and would pay whatever price they had to pay for real freedom; (3) to make men know that victory from empirical and spiritual oppression was a real possibility for all.

Jesus was not a zealot. He did not enter Jerusalem at the head of an army on Palm Sunday because his particular calling forbade him to do so. Yet he struck a fatal blow against oppression. This was his tactic. His injunction to respond to evil with good reminds us first of the freedom we possess while being oppressed.

If we will take thought, we have possession of our minds. Hatred corrupts, righteous hatred no less than unrighteous hatred. It distorts the mind and gnaws at the lining of the stomach. Jesus says: Do not cooperate in your own destruction. You know you are a man, and you know your oppressor is no more than that. Both of you are in the hands of God. Do not forget it. Love your oppressor, that is, will for him his fulfillment as a man, not as a god. By so doing, you do more than he asks and so correct him. Jesus is here concerned about the freedom of the oppressed and saving him, not first of all converting the oppressor. You have right and God on your side. Hatred is born of insecurity. You are safe. Act like it. Some men will see and be converted by it.

When he says, "Overcome evil with good," he may have in mind converting evil men, that is to say, killing them with kindness so to speak. More fundamentally, he means to pull the sting of evil for yourself.

Secondly, when Jesus speaks of turning the other cheek, going the second mile, giving more than is unjustly required, he is using Hebraic hyperbole to remind us to forgive men, not to hold grudges against them. He is saying that willing the fulfillment of the other person means not keeping track of his faults or offenses or counting them against him. Why? Because past offenses block the road to the future.

If you expect people to do evil, that expectation reinforces their evil impulses and undercuts their good impulses. Predict a thing, and the prediction helps to make it so. It's the old self-fulfilling prophecy that sociologists talk about.

Turning the other cheek is intended to wean men from sin. It means: Try the fellow again. If you trust him a second time, he may prove trustworthy. If so, it was worth it. You have assisted in his redemption.

The injunction presupposes some sort of equality, however. It presupposes not necessarily an equality of power or social standing, but at least a psychological equality which both parties recognize to some degree. Where this equality does not exist, forgiveness, giving men a second chance, too often does not reinforce their good impulses, but their bad. What should have been perceived as grace is perceived as powerless acquiescence, and what should have yielded thanksgiving yields impertinence instead.

The forgiveness of the judge whose power to do otherwise is unmistakable is quite a different matter from the forgiveness of the victim, beaten and bloodied in the street. The latter seems like the cowering of the weak before superior strength and nothing more. It is more apt to convince the beater that he may act with impunity than that he should watch his step or repent. The injunction to call no man to account, to be always open to the offender, presupposes men who perceive one another as operating on the same level and as having comparable effects on one another. Where this is not the case, turning the other cheek will confirm men in sin rather than deliver them from it [Isaiah 26:10]. Such action, far from leading to their fulfillment, must lead to their condemnation.

Never must we understand these commands against the remembrance of past offences as paralyzing us in taking action against present violation.

The oppressor is the victim of the devil, no less than the oppressed. Christian love must make that evident. The oppressor is possessed of a need to lord it over men.

He is, therefore, inadequate as a man himself. He is not the enemy. His need is.

The predominant ethical theme of the Old Testament is justice—the deliverance of men from objective oppression. That is first and fundamental. The New Testament theme is love—the deliverance of men from the need to oppress. Israel was delivered from slavery but fell herself into the trap of oppressing. God did not repent of the first act. He attacked the second.

If the oppressed is not freed from hatred, he will merely seek to subjugate the oppressor. If he is freed, he will not seek to subjugate his oppressor but to correct and equalize their relationship.

For the oppressed, the motive for action is his suffering and the suffering of others. Not just physical suffering, but the fact that it is very difficult for a person to be free of hatred while being oppressed. Jesus' message was not that oppression is good soil in which to grow integrity. Far from it. His message is: Unless you grow in integrity, you will never escape the relationship between oppressed and oppressor. You will fight and die, not for justice or equality or love, but for revenge. And the last state will then be worse than the first. Jesus died for Robert Frost's "half a revolution."

In 1966 a group of Black churchmen declared, "Powerlessness breeds a race of beggars." More recently a writer has declared that powerlessness corrupts no less than power. This is why we must act. Because oppression destroys, within and without, spiritually as well as physically.

The crime, the feelings of unworthiness and inadequacy, the internecine warfare in the Black community, these cohabit with its vibrance, its solidarity, its joy.

They are the bitter fruit of powerlessness. Crime, for instance, is the usual entry point into society of those who are upwardly mobile or wish to be but who feel shut out of that society. Petty crime is rife, and it can be traced in large part to an attempt to gain power in a community largely bereft of legitimate power.

Power makes monsters of the mighty. Powerlessness frustrates, twists, castrates, and embitters the powerless. Faulty distribution of power ruins both. To have no control over your destiny has another kind of corrupting influence than having too much power over the destinies of others, but it corrupts nonetheless.

Those with power have the means to correct the situation. Those without it must get power in order to correct the situation. But the views and possibilities of both are twisted.

The oppressed then have a responsibility to revolt, to reject oppression, for it strikes not just at their physical but their spiritual life as well.

Christian love reminds the oppressed that they possess a freedom in oppression in order that they may more successfully pursue their freedom from oppression, not as a substitute for it. Jesus never substituted "spiritual" for empirical or practical matters but considered them two faces of the same reality.

Christian love in the first instance is to will that every man may grow to the fullest extent of his capacities and enjoy "abundant life." Christian love is furthermore the willingness to take action so that what is willed may be realized. It is not love that yields no acts of love. Insofar as our calling and our situation differ from Jesus', our tactics will differ also, yet the goal is the same, and the principles that govern the action of Christians must be the same.

In the context of oppression, Christian love must first move to equalize the relationships between men. In a society, as distinguished from an individual relationship, this means that Christian love is committed to the establishment of justice. In this context, justice is the structuring of community in such a fashion that all of its members experience the opportunity for the fullest possible development of their capacities. This means, of course, that the present distortions in society must be corrected.

While it is an oversimplification, it is worth referring again to the notion that the primary concern of the Old Testament is justice and that of the New, love. They are not opposed to one another. They are, as we have said, two faces of the same head—the one general, the other particular. Similarly, they reinforce one another. In order for a just society to be structured, love—the will that all men may fulfill themselves—must be present. The goal of establishing such a society is that men may find the atmosphere suitable for the growth of such love. The establishment of a just society is intended to perpetuate such a love.

Since the inequity to which Christian love must address itself in the situation of oppression has to do first with the relationships of groups and only secondly with the relationships of individuals, Christian love's first concern is with structures rather than personal contacts, with justice rather than individual kindness. The first is a matter of right, the second a matter of personal commitment. The first is enforceable, the second commendable.

In the quest for a just society, Christian love sets itself against those forces which would perpetuate injustice and the status quo. Because of circumstances, Christian love is involved in concrete social issues first—first in energy, first in time. Yet

CHRISTIAN LOVE REQUIRES AN ACT OF IMAGINATION

the Christian's concern for his actual neighbor should not take a back seat to his concern for his "theological neighbor," the oppressed. But neither is that concern a substitute for the former.

Often Blacks have been heard to say that whites cannot know what it is like to be Black in America. The truth in this statement has tended to blind Blacks to the danger in it and let many whites off the hook.

The key to the problem is the word *know*. Of course, they cannot know. To know the experience of any other man or group requires being that man or group. The reason we can communicate at all, however, in human affairs is that we possess the faculty of imagination which permits us to duplicate parts of the experience of others.

If a man leaves his suburban home and tries to make it on the streets of Chicago or New York with what he knows and $5.00 in his pocket for a week, that is very different from having no bank account and no suburban home to return to. He may experience a panic and defenselessness for which the poor have developed survival mechanisms, but he will not participate in the hopelessness, the locked-in quality of poverty and discrimination in America. He will fail to experience the weight of centuries of "surviving," with all that that means. Yet the effort to capture this experience momentarily has value. It does not make you an expert on the experience. What it does do is expose you, however briefly, to another face of reality. The fact that you are not likely to desire more intimate acquaintance with it should tell any man

volumes about the situation of the Outs in society. In fact, this is a truism. People speak of how well welfare mothers live, but few give up their mortgaged homes and financed cars to join them if they can help it.

Whites can know what Blacks experience. If they wish, those identified with the oppressor can know what the oppressed experience because they are both human, and these experiences are common though not universal to humanity. It is just because whites can know what Blacks experience that they can be held accountable when they possess the means but fail to remedy the faults that produce this experience.

Christian love requires an act of imagination, imagination informed by knowledge. It requires not only that a person put himself in the place of another, but that he learn something about the other. About how it happens that he is in the situation he is in, about the structuring of society that works to keep him there, and about the possibilities for deliverance and how they can be brought off.

Christian love is not a feeling, but a commitment. It is an alignment with Christ, the oppressed one, in his conflict with oppression, that all men might have "abundant life." The goal of that conflict is the establishment of justice, a city in which every person may be what God ordained that he should be without unnecessary hindrance or unwarranted advantage.

Chapter 6

REDEMPTION, REPENTANCE,

AND...RECONCILIATION

We have been talking about the issue of race in this country, thinking of it in connection with salvation, creation, and original sin. We have tried to get some feel for the biblical background of oppressor and oppressed and of the way in which the Bible judges societies from the perspective of the oppressed. We have looked at the meaning of the particular setting of revelation. We have considered how the tendency that we call original sin is found in all mankind, particularly when it comes to problems relating to power, and we have seen how love and justice relate to this reality.

Now we shall look at the problem in the context of redemption, repentance, and reconciliation: To redeem something means, at root, to buy something back. We mentioned earlier the biblical year of Jubilee. If a person had lost property for some reason such as debt, in the year of Jubilee his kinsfolk had first choice upon the redemption of what had been lost.

Redemption has at its heart the meaning of restoring to the former, or better, state whether actual or mythical. The root assumption is that the former state was better than the present, that some loss or fall or deprivation has occurred between the past and the present. The fall of man from grace to sin is a mythical deprivation. The loss of property by its original owner for debt is an actual deprivation. The idea of redemption is largely objective and not necessarily moral. The cost or the effort required to achieve redemption is generally evident.

Repentance is an essentially moral and subjective concept. Its quality or its cost

to the one repenting can only be guessed. Its presence can be discovered only by its objective results. The idea of repentance presupposes that there has been a fault and that there is now a desire to straighten out that fault. In moral theology, the idea of repentance includes a feeling of guilt, sorrow for guilt, and the intent to amend life. Also, where loss has been sustained as a result of a fault, the one at fault restores what he destroyed or makes reparation (gives something in place of the thing destroyed when the loss cannot be restored, as when a life has been taken).

In order for reconciliation to become possible, redemption or repentance, or both, may be required. Reconciliation is the establishment of a relationship of harmony between parties that were at enmity.

Much of what we daily read about in the newspapers relates to the problem of redemption. The current phrase for redemption is "getting ourselves together." The Black community is trying to get itself together or to "do its thing." Part of this has to do with securing power, but part of it has to do with reclaiming a lost identity.

Redemption may be done by anyone. It is an objective reality. A slave may find a way to earn money and buy his own freedom.

A person may redeem a piece of property for a relative by buying it back. A stranger may redeem an item and return it to its original owner. The people most likely to do the redeeming, of course, are those most affected, and, in this instance of the Black experience in America, Blacks are the ones who are involved.

What is being redeemed? First of all, the past is being redeemed. Israel sought its past in the stories of Abraham, Isaac, and Jacob and in the stories of Moses. The Christian west has adopted that past.

The Black man is in quest of his past— to redeem it, to get it back so that he may save the present. Things are redeemed, after all, to make the present right in some way.

Some time ago, Daniel Patrick Moynihan published a study of the Negro family which provoked a great deal of controversy and was roundly denounced by civil rights leaders, even by men of such gentle mien as Roy Wilkins and Whitney Young. The study was not flattering to the Negro family. It detailed the rate of illegitimacy, the absent fathers, and so on. The furor was not about the details, however, but about the implication that what was needed was more social work resources instead of changes in such conditions as welfare rules, employment practices, and job training. In short, Moynihan's critics felt that what was needed was structural, rather than ameliorative, change.

The objection was based on an evaluation of the past, which Moynihan, to his credit, did not ignore but which I think he wrongly evaluated. The past, after all, if reclaimed, should strengthen our grasp on the present and our understanding of it.

If we look for the source of the troubles of the Black family, we will find its roots in the process of deculturation and the custom of breeding slaves that was embarked upon in this nation centuries ago.

The first meant that people were not only sold without regard to family ties but that families and tribes were deliberately broken up. Cohesion was discouraged because it was regarded as dangerous to discipline. Breeding, of course, also minimized social ties and made sex an economic reality rather than a social bond.

After emancipation, landless serfs, devoid of any economic base, trying to make ends meet, could hardly attend to the matter of rebuilding a family structure that had been systematically undercut. The problem was compounded by the urbanization of a people who were originally rural and by the social system that employed the Black woman in the home but rejected the Black man at the factory.

When the past is explored and the successes considered, the Black family is revealed as a remarkably durable institution, rather than the reverse.

To understand the present, the past must be known. But also to build a future, the past must be redeemed. For centuries, Blacks and whites were told that the Black man had contributed nothing to the march of civilization except the sweat of his brow and the strength of his arm. This idea has had its effect on the psyches of Black people as a group. Individuals have escaped it, and not a few, but the group labors still under a self-hatred and a self-suspicion which are paralyzing and destructive. In part, that hatred and suspicion derive from having only a past of ignominy and toil to look back on.

The violence done to the minds and spirits of millions by the loss of a past is as great as any violence done to them by the thousands of lynchings and the many race riots in this nation. It is more subtle than the action of the mob, but far more effective finally. It was as if the Black man had been born in the jungle, had worshiped sticks and stones, had eaten and procreated until he was enslaved, and then had worked for his betters until he was no longer needed.

Against this picture of racial profitlessness there stood in the past a few lonely, "exceptional" souls—Mary McCleod Bethune, G W Carver, Ralph Bunche.

Only recently has it been discovered or, rather, has it become generally known that Black men did not disappear (except as a peripheral problem) after emancipation until the emergence of Dr King. Only recently has it become known that the west coast of Africa, from which most of the slaves came, was the seat of several empires as substantial and as colorful in their day as any European counterpart.

≫Lost names—Songhay, Ghana, Mali, Timbuktu.

≫Trade routes through the plains and forests, commerce in salt and gold.

≫The king whose possessions of gold were so large that he tethered his horse to one nugget.

≫The pilgrimage of Mansa Musa, King of Mali, to the shrine of Islam in Mecca that was so magnificent that Moorish history has recorded it for posterity. Legend has it that the wealth that Mansa Musa carried with him, and freely spent, depressed the economy of Cairo for years after.

History is important to a people's conception of themselves. If they are to be redeemed, their history must be redeemed also. This is equally true of the white man's knowledge of the Black man. For too long he has had no recourse but to believe his own editing of history.

Those who are familiar with the Bible will recall that, after Israel returned from her captivity in Babylon, the people went through a period of consolidation and building. Out of this period came those things that stand for Judaism today—the codification of the law and the structure of the synagogue. It has been claimed that Judaism was born under Nehemiah and Ezra when the people rebuilt the city walls under seige, with a shovel in one hand and a weapon in the other [Ezra and Nehemiah, especially Nehemiah 4:17].

The Black community has gone through a long period of accommodation to others. To an increasing degree it has now turned its back on that and has begun to consolidate by working together.

People who hitherto asked, "How can I resemble those whom I do not resemble?" now ask, "Who am I?" and "How can I accentuate my difference?"

History must be redeemed. The self-respect of Black people must be reclaimed. For most of my life and for the history of the Black man in this country, the white man has been the pattern to imitate. He held the power. He was in the majority. He was inescapable. Success was measured by the degree to which the Black approximated him—in accomplishments, in physical appearance, in physical nearness to him. The slaves in the house were considered better than those in the field. Light-skinned Negroes were considered better than dark-skinned Negroes, and later those with college degrees and money were considered better than those without. The goal was escape, typified by the light-skinned Negro who could pass for white. Remember the movie *Pinky*? Those who couldn't pass were encouraged to make white friends, go to white schools, live near white people if they couldn't live with them. "Better yourself!"

The Black community, largely separated from its history and culture, bought the American individualistic dream

DRUMS, ISLAM, BLACKNESS ARE IN

more completely than any other group, with the least justification. It was thought that the way to escape the disabilities of Blackness was to deny them and become as white as possible. But that does something to a people. The mental anguish of the Pinkys of the world, who fear discovery, is a symbol of the bankruptcy of that policy.

No people have ever become very much by pretending that they are what they are not.

Today Blackness is being redeemed, rediscovered, and reclaimed. Nobody is quite sure precisely what that means. Much of it is fashion and the mere emphasis of difference for the sake of difference, but the heart of it is very serious. "Black is beautiful" is a very self-conscious motto, necessarily so, since for so long black has been identified with ugliness. White society has effectively labeled it such. A people must reject the label of ugliness and evil to survive and certainly if they are to prosper.

So Black authors are being read by Blacks, Black subjects are being painted and bought by Blacks, straightened hair has given way to Afros and cornrows, three-button suits to dashikis. Drums, Islam, Blackness are in. What was hidden is now boasted of. The term *Black* is itself significant. It is one that a large part of the community has chosen because it is different from the prevailing terms *colored, Negro, Afro-American,* which the white man has given us. More important, it is the opposite of white. It is useful precisely because it is unmistakably different, because that which is being redeemed is not merely something that was lost but something that was scorned and denigrated and of which its possessors were taught to be ashamed. This redemption involved rehabilitation.

All this is relatively new. There have been forerunners, such as the movement for African repatriation in the 19th century represented by people like Bishop Henry McNeal Turner of the AME Church or the Reverend Alexander Crummell of the Episcopal Church, both of whom believed that the destiny of Black people could be realized only in Africa. There was Marcus Garvey's Universal Negro Improvement Association early in this century, which enlisted thousands of Black people and may be called the first Black mass movement. Garvey sought to upgrade the self image of Blacks, was a critic of American racism and an advocate of an African state. But today the community has more power. The Black movement is more widespread and somehow deeper, more profound.

The word Black, of course, raises all the bugaboos that it always did in the minds of whites and many Blacks. Charges are leveled of separatism and antiintegrationism. The emphasis on Blackness, especially where it is exclusive, is called a counsel of despair, and in some sense it is.

When Martin Luther King, Jr, was alive he found himself trying to do two things: pull Black people together so they could be a fighting force, and then integrate or fan them out through the population. In short, the second was just the reverse of his first move. Stokely Carmichael and others have said, first, that this work of Dr King is useful only for certain kinds of goals and, second, why not do one thing at a time? The first thing to do was to pull Black people together to make them an effective force for the achievement of their own goals.

After 400 years, we had discovered that no individual really functions as a free agent until the group with which he is identified enters the arena of power. Black power is a way of redeeming the situation of Black America by enabling it to enter that arena. In one sense Black power is a counsel of despair because it looks at the ghettos of America in which the system confines us and says, "Let's not merely ask America to let us out. We have asked, and it has not let us go. Let's organize and make out of what was meant for evil something that is good so that, when the time comes, we will possess the power to get out and change the structures that imprisoned us."

In this context, repentance related to the moral quality of the present issue as it affects the oppressor first of all. Martin Luther King, Jr, appealed constantly to the conscience of the American people in the face of the nation's practices. He talked also about presenting the nation with a bill for 300 years of unrequited toil plus interest compounded. That was not merely rhetoric. It was a call to repentance. Pharaoh was called on to repent. The Hebrews who oppressed their countrymen were called on to repent. To repent means simply, stop doing what you are doing and don't let it happen again. The second half is variously interpreted: amendment of life, making restitution, or the more recent issue, paying reparations.

The Black Manifesto is where this issue has been most publicly raised.

On Sunday, May 4, 1969, that document was laid on the consciences of the Christians of America when James Forman, formerly head of the Student Non-Violent Coordinating Committee (SNCC) walked down the aisle of the famous Riverside Church in Manhattan and presented it. The Manifesto called for radical change in the organization of Black life in America and for the imple- mentation of quite specific proposals—a southern land bank for Black farmers,

training centers for community organiza- tion, a Black university, etc. It called for $500 million to be paid by the churches of America. The Manifesto was note- worthy because of several features:

≫1. The Manifesto was presented not to the State but to the Church because the Manifesto raised a moral issue, the issue of justice, to which the Church should address herself and because it is with the Church that God's judgment is supposed to begin.

≫2. The Manifesto required reparation. Restitution cannot be made for the lives destroyed or mangled by slavery, segrega- tion, and society's prejudices and unjust structures. In reparation something is given in place of that which has been taken away. Therefore something is required, like money for fashioning a different kind of future. (It is worth noting here that at the time of the exodus, we are told, God contributed to the economic base of his people by giving them "favor" in the eyes of the Egyptians so that the Hebrews were able to carry away the Egyptians' clothing, silver, and gold [Exodus 12:35-36].)

≫3. The Manifesto required that, as a sign of white America's intent to amend its life, she share the task of fashioning that future with those whom she has said were incapable and untrustworthy, that is, the Black community.

We know in large measure what has been the Church's response. Most of the noise focused on the denial of guilt, rather than on amendment of life.

It matters little whose forefathers did or did not literally hold slaves. It matters not at all if your parents came from Ireland or Italy after slavery had been abolished. The issue and the guilt rest not in the institution of slavery and the supposed guilt of slave owners but in the present organization of society which favors some over others because they are racially one with those who held slaves. In America it is a disadvantage to be Black —a cumulative disadvantage as far as the group is concerned. By the same token, there is a cumulative advantage in being born white. When a man profits from an injustice, knows that he has profited from an injustice, and takes no steps to correct it, he shares in the responsibility and the guilt of its continuation.

The heirs of the man who defrauded another, insofar as they continue to enjoy those ill-gotten gains without any attempt to make good the theft, continue to defraud the other.

The goal of the call to repentance is not punishment, but amendment of life— change, restitution, or reparation. The intent is to set right what is wrong and to locate responsibility for action.

Such an amendment will require that America alter her priorities. It will require the will to do it and her resources in both manpower and money. Finally it will require listening to those who have suffered at the system's hands.

In listening to some Christians speak, you would think that the Church possess- ed some special mystical method for social change. Even a hasty perusal of scripture ought to disabuse anyone of that idea. The Church does have a particular approach, however. The Christian faith has a bias in favor of the oppressed (as all established states generally have a bias in favor of the oppressor). The Christian bias dates from the salvation of Israel from Egypt. This faith always judges a society from the perspective of the victim, from the perspective of those who have the least within the system. It is from that perspective that repentance is required.

Without repentance and amendment of life, the goal of reconciliation is not achievable. It is not achievable because a wrong actually does stand in the way, a present, objective wrong: the organization of society to perpetuate the Black man's inferior status.

Reconciliation in the last analysis is a cooperative goal. As much as lies in its power, the Black community must redeem its situation. The white commun- ity must amend its life to complete that redemption. Then reconciliation will become possible—the meeting of men on equal footing with the present impedi- ments removed. Then we can get on with the business of living together (since neither of us is going anywhere) and forging the past into the possibilities of the future.

Chapter 7

THE PROBLEM OF EVIL

AND

THE CHURCH

Anyone looking at the chapter headings of this book might find the present conjunction surprising. It is not usual to lump these two together. They are so lumped because I think the response to the question of theodicy (the problem of evil) lies in the divine-human response to the rupture of creation commonly called the fall. The Church carries within it the story which is the basis of our judgment regarding the righteousness of God. The Church's mandate is to enter the field with God to do battle with those forces loose in creation which bring either his omnipotence or his righteousness into question.

Etymologically, theodicy has to do with the righteousness of God. Functionally, it has to do with the problem of evil. The issue is: How can we assert the righteousness of God in the face of evil which cannot be accounted for in terms of rational justice?

There seems to be no correlation between punishment and desert, between suffering and merit. Evil seems haphazard in distribution and frequently out of all proportion to any conceivable constructive end. William Jones [1973] at Yale Divinity School believes that theodicy is essential for a Black theology. I hold that theodicy, the problem of evil, is central to all theology.

The problem of evil is ultimately the problem of meaning. The source of the problem for man is not that there is evil. The problem is that there seems to be no reason for it, especially in its particular

expressions. It is the meaninglessness of evil that is the threat. It is this lack of purpose or reason that challenges God's righteousness. The problem of evil thus is really the problem of meaning, and that is the ultimate concern of both philosophy and theology.

This problem is a universal one, but for Black theology it has a particularly sharp bite. Jones [1973] calls the suffering of the Black community "ethnic suffering," which he says is maldistributed, enormous, and noncatastrophic. That is, suffering is concentrated in the Black community to a greater degree than in the rest of the nation. It claims a disproportionately large number among Blacks and continues from the cradle to the grave. Finally, it does not come, wreak havoc, and pass but goes on, generation after generation.

How does one make sense of this reality? Is it to be considered punishment for some ancient racial offense? For generations whites argued that Blacks were ordained to be hewers of wood and drawers of water because they were the seed, the descendants, of Ham, the son of Noah who saw the nakedness of his father and mocked his drunkenness [Genesis 9:20-22, 24-25; 10:1, 6]:

Noah was the first tiller of the soil. He planted a vineyard; and he drank of the wine, and became drunk, and laid uncovered in his tent. And Ham, the father of Canaan, saw the nakedness of his father, and told his two brothers outside. . . . When Noah awoke from his wine and knew what his youngest son had done to him, he said, "Cursed be Canaan; a slave of slaves shall he be to his brothers." . . . These are the generations of the sons of Noah. . . . The sons of Ham: Cush, Egypt, Put, and Canaan.

Clearly whatever one may think of this offense, the Hebrews are here taking care of their traditional enemies. The Canaanites are the people in the Land of Promise and around it who resisted the Hebrew conquest and whose religious and political institutions provided a constant temptation, pulling Israel from the worship of Yahweh to that of the gods of the land. Interestingly, the other sons of Ham mentioned either are or are the antecedents of other great enemies of the Israelites. Egypt stands here for itself, but also for the Philistines, who are said to be descendants of the Egyptians. Cush stands also for the Assyrians, the originators of the scorched-earth policy who ravaged the Northern Kingdom. With the possible exception of Canaan, far from being the servants of their brothers, the sons of Ham frequently enslaved them. But all of this is academic. Biblical curses no longer command the credence they did in the 19th century and before. Obviously Blacks never in any large number subscribed to such a theodicy in any case.

It is not my intention here to survey the ways in which the problem has been resolved by Blacks at this point, however useful and illuminating that task would doubtless be. One such solution will suffice to illustrate the fact that Blacks struggled with the solution and advanced tentative answers.

Henry McNeal Turner and Alexander Crummell, among others, held that God had permitted the Black man to be brought to America in order that he might become Christian and carry the faith back to Africa. Since the back-to-Africa movement attracted very few Blacks, it can be assumed that most did not subscribe to this interpretation. As a theodicy it remains deficient, for it does not explain God's prolonged toleration of the frustration of his plan and the suffering that centuries of "preparation" entailed. What this view does do is to focus the question in terms of the use to which suffering may be put, rather than to attempt to explain its origins.

What can we say about the fundamental problem? For the ancient Hebrews, the particular events surrounding the creation of their peoplehood, of their nation, provided an answer. God's righteousness was vindicated in that God delivered them from the slavery decreed by the pharaoh "who knew not Joseph" and made them a people. We have the story of their sojourn in the wilderness after that first deliverance, and it may be worth while to recall that Israel did not go from Egypt to Canaan on the Cannonball Express but wandered in the desert forty years (a long time according to the Hebrew way of speaking). Between the deliverance and the conquest of the land, then, lay many years of wandering, seeking, searching—a time so difficult that many longed for the certainties of slavery in Egypt, remembering only that food and clothing were then available, since at least their labor was of value to their oppressors.

Freedom for the Hebrew slave was no less ambiguous than for the freed man in the 1860s. The Black community has known a similar vindication of God in the Emancipation Proclamation, and similarly it has known a wilderness wandering that has not come to an end. Israel's wandering yielded a united people and a land. It does not yet appear what ours will yield.

What is clear is that, like everything else in history, God's righteousness is ambiguous. The emancipation was not the end of the slave's problems, but the beginning of new ones. Like the Hebrews of old, many freed Blacks without education, without land, without hope, longed for the fleshpots of the antebellum South and stumbled into new forms of bondage, not because they chose them, but because they had no other choice.

Yet it is worth while to remember that this experience is not unique in history or in the biblical revelation. Scholars remind us that the conflicts which are recorded in the books of Joshua and Judges were not swift and decisive as the books would indicate but dragged out over many years and required constant warfare and labor. Israel could labor on the walls of a new Jerusalem after their return from Babylon with a tool in one hand and a weapon in the other and feel at one with their father's fathers who had done the same when the land was first claimed.

The experience of the Black community is unique, but not unprecedented, and that is the first consideration. In retrospect, things fell into place for Israel. We must remember that the historical books of the Old Testament were all edited and assembled long after the events to which they refer. Israel had become briefly a great nation. She had suffered many reverses because of sin, she believed, and had always been restored by God and thus believed she would be again. This sense of fall and restoration makes the righteousness of God less unbelievable, yet it does not deal finally with the question. We have no Davidic Kingdom to look back on, just years of toil. God has preserved us, but for what?

The problem of evil is, I believe, the fundamental religious question, and as such it does not have a single logical answer. The faith in its entirety is the response to it. Part of that response is what we do with the evil we encounter. If we look at the Black experience as a whole, the web of deliverance and suffering forms a tangled network. The Black community is oppressed, which means that the suffering common to man in terms of disease, famine, natural catastrophe, and human perversity is compounded by a societal perversity, a structured engine of suffering to the workings of which the community has been subjected.

To assert that such suffering was deserved is unworthy. To assert that it is intended to instruct is absurd. It is to reason like the Air Force colonel who declared, after bombing a Vietnamese town off the face of the earth, "It was necessary to destroy it in order to save it." To assert that it is without purpose, however, is not only to deny the righteousness of God, it is to trivialize the pain of millions and their attempt to bear the inescapable with dignity. Black theology does not have any of these options, but if there is a purpose what is it?

All suffering is a mystery. Even the suffering we think we understand. What can it possibly mean to justify suffering as punishment, for instance? For some time now, the question of the death penalty has been debated across this country. If we were comfortable with the connection between suffering and punishment, there would be little debate. The practical question of the irreversibility of the death penalty in the case of error might bother us, but certainly not the question of immorality on the part of society. But this is understood by many to be the central issue. The issue is vengeance vs rehabilitation or security.

The concept of punishment may be deeply rooted in the human psyche, but penologists have virtually abandoned it as a reasonable or moral reason for maintaining a penal system. For them, at least, such a system's major function should be to rehabilitate the criminal and, while doing that or in lieu of doing that, isolate him from society and reduce the danger of his inflicting further harm.

If men are so enlightened, one must at least assume that, if punishment makes sense to God, it is in some other fashion or in some other sense than that in which man has understood it.

Suffering as instructional also has its problems. There is often no proportion between the lesson and the suffering. Getting burned may teach you fire is dangerous, but you may only sting your finger or you may get third-degree burns the first time around.

No, suffering is a mystery. It is in some sense part of the price of creating. It is woven into the web of the universe. It is malapportioned, but universal. In one of the Pauline letters the apostle speaks of *filling up* or *completing* "what is lacking in Christ's afflictions" [Colossians 1:24]. This is, I think, scripture's best clue. The wryness of the universe means not only that man may sin against his fellows and the world of nature, but that natural and unnatural suffering are apportioned without evident predetermination, as if one were to tip over a box of odds and ends and they fell mostly one place rather than another. The "fall of man" has set in motion distortions in the divine order so that the distribution of suffering or perhaps suffering itself must be redeemed.

The question then becomes: Why has God permitted a world in which suffering can become maldistributed, and what does he intend to do about it?

The answer to the first question is in some sense the answer to the second. If God is God, then the rupture called *the fall* (that is, man's falling away from God) was no surprise. Taking that possibility or that foreseen eventuality, God determined to create either because he was perverse or because he was confident that he could overcome the worst the fall could do. Christian theology has usually chosen to assert the second alternative because the first yields a meaningless universe, which is to capitulate to the problem of evil and to describe a god contrary to the Judaeo-Christian tradition.

What does God plan to do about evil? Certainly the event known as Christ is the response to that question. He intends to vindicate his own righteousness before men by enduring what he has permitted in order to overcome it. By enduring evil and identifying with man, God intends to join man and enlist him in the conflict to defeat the forces that the fall unleashed and thus create a new order. The answer to the problem of evil lies in the response we make to evil, the response consonant with God's response.

In the 9th chapter of John's gospel, Jesus and his disciples approach a man blind from birth. His disciples, men of their time, assumed his blindness to be a divine punishment and inquired if it was the man's sins or those of his parents that had caused it. Jesus replies [John 9:3-4]:

> "It was not that this man sinned, or his parents, but that the works of God might be made manifest in him."

And he anointed the man's eyes with spittle and sent him to wash, and when he did he was healed. Jesus is not here replacing one explanation with another. Certainly if he is, his explanation is worse than the disciples', for then we would have to believe that God had blinded this man from birth as a kind of stage prop so that when Jesus came along the road he could cure the man. No, what Jesus is giving is not a reason for evil but a purpose to which this suffering can be put.

The problem of evil then cannot be intellectually resolved. It is susceptible of no neat response, but it can be responded to. The offering of Christ, his identification as man and as the oppressed one means that God himself is willing to endure, is subjected to, the pain and suffering of his universe. If I may be strongly anthropomorphic, one might say that, since God does not suffer in his eternal nature the limitations of finitude, then he lacks its merits as well as its problems. That is, God's suffering is not limited by space and time or bodily weakness. It is not limited by a body. He cannot look for death to deliver him from suffering. He will not faint when it becomes too great. He chose it. He must bear it all.

The offering of Christ asserts that God is a responsible architect. That does not answer the question, but it is good to know. That offering also asserts that he will win out, that men will overcome the powers that oppress and the drives that lead men to need to oppress other men.

The resurrection is a theodicy, a vindication of God's righteousness, because it declares that it is not possible for the good to die forever or for the divine will to be finally frustrated. The resurrection empowered the Church to be, to rise from the death of loss and meaninglessness to life. It enabled the Church to identify God with the insulted and injured and itself to join the oppressed in a battle it is confident of winning.

All this does not answer the question: Why is there suffering in the world in general and why is there ethnic suffering in particular? What it does do is put the answer in a context.

I had a teacher once who used to say that, if you dismiss the problem of evil, then you have the problem of good. What he meant was that, looking at the evidence for evil, the amount, severity, and extent of it, you may be tempted to say that the universe is meaningless and evil, without purpose, random. That delivers one from the necessity of explaining it. Then the problem is: What do you do with the good, with the fortitude and grace in suffering, with love and hope and courage and all the other things we commend? In a meaningless, random world, the good things, too, must be meaningless and random. The reason there is a problem of evil is that we must make some sense of the good, and evil threatens any easy sense we can make of good. The problem of good insists that the universe must have meaning.

The Black community in its darkest days has insisted that the universe had meaning. Otherwise, how could it bear its suffering? It is precisely the oppressed who bear witness to God's righteousness, because it is right, because frequently it is the only right thing they know.

If there is to be no vindication, no salvation, what is it all for? The problem of evil in whatever form it appears is the quest for meaning. Men do not make meaning in the universe, but they contribute to it. If they give it up, what will be the point of the universe's continuance, at least as it is related to them? There is an old saying: "The blood of the martyrs is the seed of the Church." The point is that nothing can grow if no one is willing to die for it. The universe is a costly affair. I think that can be shown without too much difficulty. The endurance of suffering is apparently a part of that cost.

It is not to be suffered meekly, but in the pursuance of integrity, inevitably.

Jesus is often represented as meekly submitting to suffering. A closer reading of scripture ought to convey a quite different impression. When he prayed in the garden for the cup of sorrow to pass, he was being quite human. It was man's business to avoid pain and suffering, but not at the cost of his integrity. Jesus accepted his suffering because he recognized he could not avoid it without sacrificing his integrity.

He had a task. It was not to suffer, but to be faithful to his destiny. What he suffered was as essential and as incidental as the ground you traverse when you go on a journey. That ground, however, is in no sense why you go.

Only fools seek suffering, but only cowards betray themselves in order to avoid it. The suffering of a soldier is part of the game, and the distribution is random, but the presence of suffering is not. Suffering is the cost, not of the conflict, but of the goal. This is what Paul is talking about, I think, when he speaks of "filling up the sufferings of Christ."

It is as if a great boulder slipped from its perch and overhangs the city. To right it will take the labors of thousands, straining, pushing, bruised, and hurt. The people who dwell in the city are enlisted to help. Some volunteer, some are cajoled, some driven, some just happen by. Some shirk and escape. When the boulder is righted, we shall know who did it and who did not. Then it will matter more that you did it than why. Thus men must say whether they will contribute the suffering they did not seek to that needed to right the world, or vote for meaninglessness and night.

The creation of the world was a divine risk. Redeeming it is too. Man was not consulted in its creation, but he must be in its redemption, else it cannot finally be redeemed. That is part of the meaning of human freedom. That is the divine risk. The Church is supposed to be that community which has thrown its lot in with God, which is prepared to call its suffering by his name, to identify as he has with the oppressed.

Scripture abounds in images of the Church. Some stress the fact that it is a congregation or community of faith, that is to say, of those who stand with God and his work over against the powers of evil. Traditionally faith has been set in opposition to works. The distinction is logical but functionally absurd. What a man really believes determines what he does. If he believes God is for the oppressed, he will not only say so but he will take his place with them.

One central image of the Church is that of the body of Christ. The fundamental implication of this is the old Anglican formula that the Church is "the extension of the Incarnation." It is the visible body, the means whereby the risen Lord continues his work in creation. He is no less in need of arms and feet and tongues than he was before. The work of Christ, then, is the work of the Church. Its task is to be identified with those whom the world hates so that it may bring the world to love. Christ has completed his work in principle. Now it falls to the Church to appropriate that work and to live it out in the world in fact.

As Christ was visible in the body, so is the Church visible, and as the work of Christ was visible, the work of the Church should be. Christ's challenging of the powers of evil took tangible form in the healing of the sick, the cleansing of the possessed, the raising of the dead, the challenge to the pious and the mighty, and the proclamation of deliverance to the poor. The work of the Church is also to take tangible form and along similar lines.

The Church's task is different from that of Christ in that it can undertake in knowledge what he undertook, so to speak, in faith. He tackled the powers of evil without knowing the outcome. We know, for he has gone before us.

The body of Christ implies that the spirit of God indwells the Church and that it is as he is because his spirit dwells in it. If Christ is Black,* then his Church must be as certainly as he is.

The Church is the eschatological community,† the community oriented to the end, that is to say, oriented not just to the end of history but to the end of a job. The Church is oriented toward accomplishment, not just to fidelity, although, if faith is thought of as active instead of passive, fidelity is clearly seen to be oriented toward accomplishment, to an end. The disciples believed that Christ rose from the dead precisely because he was the kind of person it could be believed of. His life and work make his great work believable in retrospect. Had he not shown mastery in life over the evils of disease and madness, no one would have believed his mastery over the last enemy, death, and its shadow—meaningless. By the same token, unless the Church tackles the hard tasks, aligns itself with those who suffer and undertakes to vanquish the enemies of God, it will not matter how many baptisms are performed, how many receive the sacrament of Holy Communion. Baptism, the Eucharist will be only dumb show, for these acts, the sacraments, are supposed to show forth not an intangible but a tangible spiritual change. They are

*See Chapter 7 for the concept of the Black Christ.
†See Chapter 7.

supposed to empower men to take arms against real evil. The Church is supposed to equip and motivate men in the art of the war with evil, evil not only in the private places of their hearts, but evil in the world where men groan under the weight of ignorance, hunger, pain and oppression.

If the Church has no accomplishments to its credit now, who will believe it can bring off its promise hereafter? The issue is credibility. Jesus was credible. Is his Church? The community of hope is not supposed to be selling a product whose total claim is available only after it is purchased.

Men do not hope because there is nothing else to do and in spite of everything. Men can hope in spite of much. If there were nothing to count against hope, there would be no need for it. But if nothing counts in its favor, who will have the gall to advocate it? If the Church hopes, she will act on that hope and somewhere groans will cease, health will return, the crushed will stand upright as a result. That is why we can say that, where men are liberated, there is God, and the instrument of that liberation is his Church, however it may understand itself, for it does his work in the world. It is his body, if only for a day.

The Church hopes for a city, but who will commission an architect to lay out a city who has not a house or office building to his credit? She hopes for a city where men will live in harmony as they live in disharmony now, where they will live in health as they suffer now from pain and disease, where they will know as now they ignorantly labor, where they will stand as equals as now they are subjected to one another.

Many men see the here and the hereafter as set in opposition: The by-and-by is nothing; the here-and-now is all. This is a natural reaction to a lot of things.

Among Blacks, at least, not the least is the attempt to make the oppressed feel content with their earthly lot in expectation of a kingdom to come. The oppressors enjoyed their goods and the goods of the oppressed and promised the oppressed benefits which God would have to pay for.

In fact, the meaning of life cannot be exhausted by life itself. It is bearable only because we may believe that God will be vindicated, that the mysterious will be made known, that the world's laboring and suffering have an end which is good and in which all who bear the pain of it will share. The Church's final hope is that meaning will be unequivocably demonstrated and the universe redeemed. No one will subscribe to such a hope, however, unless it can be seen that that hope motivates action.

For any fool can see that, if we really believe that God stands against evil and oppression and that he will win out and that that is what the whole shooting match is about, then those who believe are free men already. They are liberated already. They can risk all because they risk nothing. For whatever they lose will be restored a thousandfold. Any fool can also see that insofar as we do not act, we do not believe, and just so far is our hope shown to be a sham and Christ's work denied.

Fundamental to the biblical view of the Church is, of course, that it is the people of God, the people who know liberation and creation first hand and, knowing, trust God to make a way. But perhaps even more importantly they join him in making that way. They are the people who are on edge with the world. They are the "strangers and sojourners on the

earth,"* seeking a city unlike any that has yet been raised. They are on edge with the world, the gadflies, the revolutionaries, for whom good is never good enough. They are the oppressed who have made their oppression a calling, who have made their particular experience a window into universal man.

Certainly no community in America knows better what it means to be a community of hope than the Black community.

Certainly no community in America knows better what it means to be strangers and sojourners in the only land they know, a land which covers the bones of their fathers and their father's fathers for a decade of generations and beyond, and which still is strange.

No one knows better what it means to be on edge with the world.

For the Church this is not simply a circumstance. It is a vocation. To champion the oppressed is to have no continuing city. But this is what it is all about, for the Church's Lord, too, had no place to lay his head. For no army can be comfortable until the war is won and to be the people of God in the midst of the world is to be salt, to be leaven, to be an army committed to change, to change as real as seasoning, as visible as rising bread, as central as liberation. This is the Church's mission, and her mission is the essence of her nature and her life.

*For example, Exodus 22:21; 23:9; Leviticus 19:33; 25:23; Deuteronomy 10:18; 23:7; 24:14; 1 Chronicles 29:15; Psalm 39:12.

Chapter 8

... RECONCILIATION *(continued)*

THE LAST THINGS

Our intention has been twofold: to look at one of the pressing problems of our time, *the* pressing problem for this nation, and to use our consideration of the issues it raises to illuminate our understanding of the faith we profess. So far we have dealt with this problem in the light of Christian teaching. This last chapter is no exception.

Since it is the last chapter, we shall view it from the standpoint of what the Church calls the last things, the consummation, the goal or fulfillment of all things.

The chapter is entitled "Reconciliation" and subtitled "The Last Things" in order to point out that there is an analogy between the final fulfillment of the human enterprise and the fulfillment in time of any particular aspect of that enterprise. It is not always easy to keep them separate because the final hope inspires the realization of particular goals, and the accomplishment of particular goals is a foretaste of the final hope and a guide to it.

Having said that, we proceed with the intention of seeing how the final hope illuminates the particular goal of racial reconciliation.

If you look at the back of a one dollar bill, you will see pictured the two sides of the great seal of the United States. The obverse contains the promise *Novus Ordo Seclorum.* When you spend money, look at that sometime.

The founding fathers of our country were aware of the scriptural associations of the word *new.* They herald a period of fulfillment, of justice and brotherly love.

> Behold, I make all things new [Revelation 21:5].
> A new heaven and a new earth [Revelation 21:1; Isaiah 65:17].
> A new heart I will give you, and a new spirit I will put within you [Ezekiel 36:26].

They proposed to found on these shores "a new order of the ages"—a social organization that would be the fulfillment of the promised harmony of man, frustrated on the continent of Europe but to be realized in this new land. It was to be a preview of the New Jerusalem into which scripture tells us all peoples were welcome and to which all would bring their particular contributions, in which grew a tree, the leaves of which were for the healing of their historical wounds.

The language is the language of the end time, the consummation, when things will be as God intended them to be, not as they are now. But the new order rapidly began to adjust to the old. Thomas Jefferson's paragraph condemning the slave trade and, by implication, slavery itself was dropped from the Declaration of Independence. The new order was shoved right back behind the same old eight ball by the constitutional exclusion of Blacks, not only from citizenship but from personhood, by making them, for purposes of determining the number of a state's representatives, count as three-fifths of a man.

Yet the image was sound. The new order requires reconciliation—the acceptance of every one as he is, every man and every group. The biblical picture of the New Jerusalem is one of variety: All nations bring their gifts, and the old wounds and quarrels are healed.

Variety is the keynote.

But our new order of the ages prides itself on sameness, on conformity. The first thing that must change for the fulfillment of the promise, at least as it affects the relations of the races, is that America must become tolerant of variety. This nation still, despite its TV commercials, considers itself a white nation. It is not. In fact, it never has been. Before Jamestown, there were the Indians; afterwards, the Blacks and the Indians, the Orientals and the Puerto Ricans. Either we shall learn tolerance of variety or our tendencies toward Fascism will overwhelm us.

There is an organization in my community which exists to alert Black people to the plans made for them by the government. These plans include a strategic network of highways to move troops and to divide people, a system of concentration-camp sites, a list of leaders to be interned (since you can't intern 23 million people), and other such measures. The people who give out this information believe it. They are convinced by what they have learned that the planned consummation, the end time, will be the withdrawal of the promise and a reaffirmation of America's image of itself as a white nation.

You don't believe this treatment awaits the Black community? One white clergyman of prominence, upon hearing of these plans for controlling the Blacks commented, "I don't believe it!— But I wouldn't be surprised."

It is significant that, while the suburbs think of the greatest danger to our society as coming from the left, the Black community sees the promised new order of God as falling before the forces of the right, whose slogan is now "law and order" with no mention of justice.

The fulfillment of the promise will require a society that is sincerely tolerant of difference. This nation made one solution of the problem of difference which has been disastrous for it. It is a solution that is quite human but also quite destructive: the ingroup-outgroup solution. We seem incapable of noting difference without asking, "Which is better?" and "Which is worse?"—without specifying for what. Difference, at least in the American mind, seems inextricably bound to the question of inferior and superior. A rose is not a chrysanthmum— but which is better? or worse?

Recently the new phenomenon Black theology has appeared in the churches. Actually the newest thing about the phenomenon has been its name. In this book we have been looking at some of this. Black theology is, so far at least, simply the theological interpretation of the Black experience. That task, as was pointed out in the first chapter, has been going on for some time.

C L Franklin, the father of Aretha Franklin, the singer, tells a story of the origin of a spiritual. He says that one of the Wesleys came to the States to preach, and the slaves all went to hear him. Because of the number of people who turned out, the slaves were excluded from their usual place in the gallery and had to stand outside at the windows. After the sermon, the altar call was issued. One old lady named Mary was so moved that she walked into the church and up to the altar and indicated that she wanted to join the church. She was refused. When she insisted, she was told to go join one of her own churches. She turned tearfully and walked down the aisle mumbling, "I'm going to tell God, one of these days, how you treat me." The slaves, standing outside witnessing this scene, began to sing

Oh, Mary, don't you weep
Don't you mourn,
Pharaoh's army got drownded.

Either that spiritual is an instance of Black theology or that story is.

The theologizing of the Black experience is important, not only for the Black people, but for white people as well. James Cone [1969], in his book entitled *Black Theology and Black Power,* says there is no church but the Black church, no Christ but the Black Christ. He means by that that the Church is the Church only when it champions oppressed people. In this time and in this country, the symbol of the oppressed is Blackness.

Right now there is some talk in the Black community about the images in the Black church—images (pictures or statues) still teach, of course. It has been asserted that Christ should be shown as Black since every people depict him as their own and because white Christs imply that God is white and encourage the traditional subservience of Black people to whites, who occupy all other seats of authority. It is pointed out that, whatever Jesus of Nazareth looked like, he looked no more like the pale Galilean nordic whom we usually see in pictures than he did like the Black Louisiana roustabout. One wag has commented that this first-century Jew certainly looked more like Groucho Marx than like Herman Mellvile's pale and tongue-tied Billy Budd.

Consider this matter for a moment for it provides us with another clue to the Church's past work and its present opportunity. Until recently, an observer would be hard put to find Christ portrayed as Black in a Black church. There are at least two reasons for this. One is that white people make most of the church windows, statuary, etc, and they make him like themselves. But there is a more important reason. Before we consider it, though, let me make a relevant observation.

Most Black churches are named for or in relation to Black people. The name "African" figured prominently in the names of many churches before the days of integration encouraged churchmen to prematurely remove it. Episcopal churches are usually named for St Philip, the Jew who converted the Ethiopian eunuch, or for Augustine or Cyprian, bishops in North Africa. Hosts of African Methodist Episcopal churches bear the name Allen for the founder, Richard Allen, who left the Methodist church after he was dragged from his knees while worshiping in a church of that denomination. Black parishes and Black denominations usually owe their foundation to similar experiences, yet hardly ever is Christ depicted in them as Black. The reason, I believe, is that as a group the Black community has never completely accepted itself. We have been Christ's children, but not his friends. We have loved him and perhaps because we have loved him we have not permitted him to be one of us and share our suffering though, as a people, we have shared his.

There is an old slave story that says all people were born black. Then one day all were told to go wash in the Jordan where they would turn white and have the kinks taken out of their hair. Some did and became white. Others sat on the fence and watched and laughed until they saw whether it worked, but, by then, all the water had been used up except for enough to wash the palms of their hands and the soles of their feet.

The story reveals the humor that has helped Black people survive. It reveals somebody's view of the faults of that community. But most of all it reveals the belief that it is better to be white. Not only has Blackness been equated with folly and suffering, but it is objectively, inherently better to have a white skin and straight hair. To depict Jesus as Black, then, would be neither a compliment nor a consolation. It would not be a compliment to him because he would be made equal to an inferior man. It would not be a consolation to his followers because who would follow an inferior being if a superior were available?

Until recently, you would be hard put to find Christ represented as Black in Black churches in America because we were not able to say, "The best thing I can do for my friend is to make him one with myself." The American Indian, an oppressed minority, still considers it their highest honor to take a man into their tribe. But Christ has not been taken into ours. Yet Christ *is* Black. He affirms our identity as we are. If the gospel means anything to Black people, it must mean at least that. The self-hatred in the Black community is the heritage of slavery and the white cultural, social, and economic domination that followed.

But a new day is dawning. A rediscovery of history, of worth, of a style and a meaning peculiar to the Black community is changing all that.

It is a sound instinct that leads men to represent Christ as one of themselves, as a friend. The love we have for others can only be a sick love if we have none for ourselves.

But Christ never comes simply as a friend. He did not 2000 years ago, and he does not now. He divides men. He comes to move and change men. Yes, he affirms who they are—first. But he comes

also to make them what they should be. He comes as judge. As one teacher has noted, Jesus was not crucified for saying, "Consider the lillies of the field," but for showing up the respectable people and for threatening the people in power. He came as a friend, but at the same time as judge. You either changed and kept him as a friend or you refused and made him become, for you, an enemy.

So, while it is natural to represent Christ as one of our own, whoever we may be, it is dangerous too, for we may be lulled into believing that, since he is a friend, it ends there, when in reality that is where it begins. Christ comes as judge, as someone different, foreign to us, inviting, demanding change. He comforts but he also chastizes. Often we do not recognize him or understand the company he keeps. The Risen Christ goes where Jesus went— to the outsiders, to those whom society has rejected. In Judea he went to those who did not live up to the high standards of a time-consuming religion—to prostitutes, cheats, and the simple people of the land. In Nazi Germany he went about with a star of David sewn on his coat as a Jew—because then they were outsiders, the symbol and victims of oppression. In India he is an untouchable and, in America, he is Black. Wherever the sickness of society surfaces, there he is, demanding that we deal with it—a friend, loving us, but a judge because he loves us all. He forces us to deal with what we'd rather avoid. He is suddenly hard and foreign where he has been gentle and friendly, forcing us to act because he himself becomes the outcast, the untouchable, the Jew, the Black. He makes us scorn, ignore, shove aside, kill or accept him, in the form of the one whom society has locked out of its goods and its life.

Christ is Black because Blackness is America's sickness, its outsider, the reality it would rather ignore or destroy. Christ is Black because white America excludes Blackness, and Black America has been taught to be ashamed of it.

That is why in every church in America Christ should in some prominent place be shown as Black so that men will remember that he is not simply our friend—ours is not a religion of the status quo—but that this is also the strange God, the judging, redeeming God who requires of us that we conform to his will and the breath of his love. Then it would be visually clear that a person who does not love his strange brother cannot love Christ either.

In this way we would be assisting in escaping the pietistic approach to religion which has been the bane of American religion. Rather than emphasizing our personal piety, we could begin to think in terms of the incarnation—in terms of what it means that God became man.

For at heart, when we speak of the incarnation, or the embodiment, of God, we mean that he participated fully in human life—personal life and life in society, just as we do. His interests are then both individual and universal. He speaks to personal morality and to price control, to interpersonal relations and to the relations of structures and groups. When we say that God became flesh, we mean that he became part of the picture, enmeshed in life, all of it as we are, yet, because he was God, bringing judgment and making demands upon us for change, not because of what he said but because of who he was. He is one of us, but he is not us. Near us, yet strange to all not willing to subscribe to his point of view.

We need also, therefore, to use a new definition of the word *spiritual.* People come to the church for peace and quiet. They are therefore outraged when they encounter demand for action and sermons that deal with the difficult issues that the world faces. They have been given a too easy distinction between Church and World, between Awe and Action. There is little wonder that the Church has fallen either into one fault or the other.

The idea of the incarnation establishes a tension, a tension that is difficult to maintain constructively without the presence of the incarnate one, Jesus Christ.

I do not mean to oversimplify the problem or the solution, but incarnation implies that there is no simple distinction between church and world. Rather, the distinction is to be worked out with fear and trembling: Awe infuses secular things, and the secular surrounds the awesome. The awesome God makes moral demands. It behooves us to look at church activity to see if, beyond our claim, we can really see that it is an activity in which God is interested or involved or if we have, in our eagerness for our own concerns, gotten too far from his activity in the world.

Finally, the consummation, the establishment of the new order, if and when it comes, will be founded by those born in the wilderness, just as was true of Israel's entrance into the Promised Land. Dr Thomas Kilgore, former President of the American Baptist Convention, made this point on one occasion when he was talking about Black people. Let me apply it to Blacks and whites. He was saying that he had been asked to write an article on the militant Blacks, and he titled the article, "Judgment Reserved." He reserved judgment because, he said, last year's radical is this year's conservative. Even though the new young radicals were doing things he had never dreamed of, he recognized that he had "the taint of slavery." That is, he came from a generation that had known segregation and been formed in it.

Like the Hebrews newly freed from Egypt, many now living have murmured against the Lord, saying, "Why did you bring us into this desert?" Now, as then, they long for the fleshpots of Egypt, preferring a full belly to freedom.

Daily we hear the present period of transition deplored. Blacks and whites long for what is mistakenly called the good old days, before polarization, before separation, before riots, before agitation. It was Frederick Douglass who said the people who want change without agitation are like those who want rain without lightning and thunder, who want crops without plowing up the ground.

Those who long for the fleshpots of Egypt will participate in the journey, but they will not see the land of promise. For, as a parable, Kilgore reminded us that only two of those who came out of Egypt entered the Land of Canaan. The rest died in the desert. The generation that received the fulfillment of the promise were those born in the desert, unspoiled by the old master-slave relationship. They were born free.

It is to that generation that the consummation belongs if it is to come at all. That consummation presupposes the Black community's redemption of its identity and the white community's repentance of its denial, which will make the reconciliation possible.

Christians are assured that the end of history will be fulfillment, healing, and peace. But no such assurance obtains with regard to historical problems. In history we have a choice, for history is the arena of human freedom. In the end, God's will will prevail, but in history it can be frustrated. In history the alternatives are fulfillment or judgment. If there is no redemption or no repentance, there can be no reconciliation.

The divine bias remains, and the oppressor cannot escape the judgment, for sooner or later the conflict must be resolved. Whether in Israel's departure from Egypt and the death of the first born or in the New Jerusalem, the choice remains, in history, in the hands of men.

We come now to the conclusion of this book. My intention has been to lift up some of the salient points with which Black theology is concerned, give some background on them, and make some constructive comments. The reader now understands that I was serious when I entitled this effort a primer. It is in no sense an exhaustive or even a systematic presentation.

I mentioned earlier that Black theology was a theology of liberation. I wish to finish by drawing some conclusions from that fact that relate to its future development.

Without overstating the case, it may be said that the Black revolution is a conservative revolution. It began by a people asking in—in on the current thing, actual American society. Of all the immigrant groups that have gone to make up this land, none has had a greater investment in it and none is more American than the Black community.

The Black man was brought to these shores more than a century before the republic was framed. The culture, religion, social life that he possessed were systematically destroyed and only partially replaced by the Anglo-Saxon culture, most of which he had to personally adapt to his own particular circumstances in this land. His present culture owes less to his homeland and more to America than that of any other identifiable ethnic group, and he forged it on this soil. It may validly claim the designation American. For two centuries, he mixed his blood, sweat, and tears with the soil, planted and harvested crops, and built capital so that a great nation might grow rich, but he himself had no share in those rewards.

No one except the American Indian has a better claim to be in America than he. But gradually as the "legitimate" means, the accepted means, for change were exhausted, he began to conclude that this society was not designed for him. The doors that opened for Poles and Greeks, for Jews and Slovaks did not open for him. From criticizing men for not letting him into the going thing, he began to see that the thing itself needed to be criticized. The new order of the ages had great promise, but it hadn't come off.

It was not America's entry ports which needed to be changed. America itself needed to be changed. A new vision was required of that new order that is spoken of on our $1 bill—a new vision that welcomed pluralism, that could accommodate and appreciate difference. So the conservative revolution became radicalized. That process has not stopped.

The ripples in the pond have begun to spread. Echoes return from unexpected quarters, crying for a new vision, for a new understanding of God's dispensation and his will for human liberation.

Nikki Giovanni, the Black poetess, is reputed to have said of the feminist revolution that it was an argument between Mr Charlie and Miss Ann, and the maid had better stay out of it. But the argument won't go away, and increasingly the maid will be getting into it, with her own perspective, but into it nonetheless.

The feminists have scaled the theological walls, not only on issues like ordination, but on much more fundamental issues like the patriarchal bias of scripture. They have called for and begun a renovation of our language and theological imagry. They are not going away.

Pierre Berton [1965] in his book *The Comfortable Pew*, somewhere observed that the closest contemporary analogue to the "outcasts" whom Jesus consorted with is the homosexual. Homosexuals provoke the same emotionally charged antipathy today that freighted the words "sinner" or "outcast" then.

Interestingly, other writers have just as cogently made the argument using the word "nigger." It is worth noting that homosexuals enjoy the same kind of discriminatory legal attention that Blacks have enjoyed, although within a more limited sphere. They are still subject to the social opprobrium with which Blacks are familiar. The gay revolution has completed the call for a new understanding theologically as well as socially of the roles of the sexes and of sex. Like the feminists', it raises questions about the cultural conditioning of scripture and the nature of revelation.

The similarities of oppressed groups are as numerous as, of course, are their differences. The thing that really relates them is the thrust for integrity and liberation. They all demand a different vision of the new order than what now obtains. They all require a different, more perceptive appreciation of the biblical revolution and a new appreciation of the divine activity in history.

The angles are different and unfortunately have often proved conflicting.

Black theology is still in the developmental stages, but I think it can no longer ignore the other theologies of liberation that are arising. While its perspective and experience are different, yet, if truth is a whole, they must be related.

The Black revolution must be as wary of being played off against these movements as it should be of being played off against Red power or Brown power.

Although the interests of all these groups are varied, their claims must be heard. One of the ploys of the oppressor is to throw a stone into our midst and let us kill one another for him. Oppression does not make men or women noble. It makes them fearful, insecure, and distrustful—the kinds of feelings to which the gospel also speaks. If we are to realize the liberation we seek, we must demonstrate the possibility of plural approaches which are open to each other, share a common vision, and reinforce each other.

Major Jones [1971] is right when he says God is not on our side: we are on his if we are for liberation. For one thing is evident, liberation comes at different levels and in different ways. God has raised up hosts. It falls to us to coordinate those hosts into an army, to establish understandings, to form coalitions so that our vision may become the vision of the future.

This is a task to which Black theologians must be open. It must be done. If it is, we should expect it to prove a source of enrichment as well as liberation, an earnest of a new order, a really new order yet to come.

APPENDICES

Preface

The civil rights movement of the 1950s and the 1960s occasioned major changes in American life. It also provoked those who participated and those who watched to reexamine in the light of that crisis their understanding of the racial situation in the nation. Christians reviewed their theological assumptions, the nature of the institutions in which they lived and served, and the shape of their future commitments.

The phenomenon called Black theology in part originated and was in part affirmed and reenforced by this reflection. Black theology is not the preserve or the pet of a few, but part of a movement. It is part of a movement among churchmen which produced the National Committee of Black Churchmen, the only national inter-denominational organization of Black clergy in America. It is part of a movement which has yielded Black caucuses in all the major predominately white churches. It is part of a movement which is interdenominational, Christian, and Black and which seeks to respond to the the perceived realities of oppression in America and beyond from a Christian perspective.

In order to illustrate the nature of this movement, as part of this primer we have appended some "original sources," documents produced by churchmen struggling with the themes and motifs which have yielded Black theology.

They are of various types, from open letters to the nation to rationales for doing a "Black thing" in a white setting. This material is pulled together here to provide background for the general reader and, for the scholar, source material not readily available elsewhere. No attempt has been made to provide exhaustive coverage of this material but, rather, to illustrate some of the origins, implications, and concerns of that ferment of which Black theology is both an outcome and a guide.

APPENDIX A

"BLACK POWER"

A Statement by the National Committee of Negro Churchmen
July 31, 1966

We, an informal group of Negro churchmen in America, are deeply disturbed about the crisis brought upon our country by historic distortions of important human realities in the controversy about "black power." What we see shining through the variety of rhetoric is not anything new but the same old problem of power and race which has faced our beloved country since 1619.

We realize that neither the term "power" nor the term "Christian Conscience" is an easy matter to talk about, especially in the context of race relations in America. The fundamental distortion facing us in the controversy about "black power" is rooted in a gross imbalance of power and conscience between Negroes and white Americans. It is this distortion, mainly, which is responsible for the widespread,

66

though often inarticulate, assumption that white people are justified in getting what they want through the use of power, but that Negro Americans must, either by nature or by circumstances, make their appeal only through conscience. As a result, the power of white men and the conscience of black men have both been corrupted. The power of white men is corrupted because it meets little meaningful resistance from Negroes to temper it and keep white men from aping God. The conscience of black men is corrupted because, having no power to implement the demands of conscience, the concern for justice is transmuted into a distorted form of love, which, in the absence of justice, becomes chaotic self-surrender. Powerlessness breeds a race of beggars. We are faced now with a situation where conscienceless power meets powerless conscience, threatening the very foundations of our nation.

Therefore, we are impelled by conscience to address at least four groups of people in areas where clarification of the controversy is of the most urgent necessity. We do not claim to present the final word. It is our hope, however, to communicate meanings from our experience regarding power and certain elements of conscience to help interpret more adequately the dilemma in which we are all involved.

I. To the Leaders of America:
Power and Freedom

It is of critical importance that the leaders of this nation listen also to a voice which says that the principal source of the threat to our nation comes neither from the riots erupting in our big cities, nor from the disagreements among the leaders of the civil rights movement, nor even from mere raising of the cry for "black power." These events, we believe are but the expression of the judgment of God upon our nation for its failure to use its abundant resources to serve the real well-being of people, at home and abroad.

We give our full support to all civil rights leaders as they seek for basically American goals, for we are not convinced that their mutual reinforcement of one another in the past is bound to end in the future. We would hope that the public power of our nation will be used to strengthen the civil rights movement and not to manipulate or further fracture it.

We deplore the overt violence of riots, but we believe it is more important to focus on the real sources of the eruptions. These sources may be abetted inside the ghetto, but their basic causes lie in the silent and covert violence which white middle-class America inflicts upon the victims of the inner city. The hidden, smooth and often smiling decisions of American leaders which tie a white noose of suburbia around the necks, and which pin the backs of the masses of Negroes against the steaming ghetto walls—without jobs in a booming economy; with dilapidated and segregated educational systems in the full view of unenforced laws against it; in short: the failure of American leaders to use American power to create equal opportunity *in life* as well as *in law*—this is the real problem and not the anguished cry for "black power."

From the point of view of the Christian faith, there is nothing necessarily wrong with concern for power. At the heart of the Protestant reformation is the belief that ultimate power belongs to God alone and that men become most inhuman when concentrations of power lead to the conviction—overt or covert—that any nation, race or organization can rival God in this regard. At issue in the relations between whites and Negroes in America is the problem of inequality of power. Out of this imbalance grows the disrespect of white men for the Negro personality and community, and the disrespect of Negroes for themselves. This is a fundamental root of human injustice in America. In one sense, the concept of "black power" reminds us of the need for and the possibility of authentic democracy in America.

We do *not* agree with those who say that we must cease expressing concern for the acquisition of power lest we endanger the "gains" already made by the civil rights movement. The fact of the matter is, there have been few substantive gains since about 1950 in this area. The gap has constantly widened between the incomes of non-whites relative to the whites. Since the Supreme Court decision of 1954, de facto segregation in every major city in our land has increased rather than decreased. Since the middle of the 1950s unemployment among Negroes has gone up rather than down while unemployment has decreased in the white community.

While there has been some progress in some areas for equality for Negroes, this progress has been limited mainly to middle-class Negroes who represent only a small minority of the larger Negro community.

These are the hard facts that we must all face together. Therefore we must not take the position that we can continue in the same old paths.

When American leaders decide to serve the real welfare of people instead of war and destruction; when American leaders are forced to make the rebuilding of our cities first priority on the nation's agenda; when American leaders are forced by the American people to quit misusing and abusing American power; then will the cry for "black power" become inaudible, for the framework in which all power in America operates would include the power and experience of black men as well as those of white men. In that way, the fear of the power of each group would be removed. America is our beloved home-

land. But, America is not God. Only God can do everything. America and the other nations of the world must decide which among a number of alternatives they will choose.

II. To White Churchmen:
Power and Love

As black men who were long ago forced out of the white church to create and to wield "black power," we fail to understand the emotional quality of the outcry of some clergy against the use of the term today. It is not enough to answer that "integration" is the solution. For it is precisely the nature of the operation of power under some forms of integration which is being challenged. The Negro Church was created as a result of the refusal to submit to the indignities of a false kind of "integration" in which all power was in the hands of white people. A more equal sharing of power is precisely what is required as the precondition of authentic human interaction. We understand the growing demand of Negro and white youth for a more honest kind of integration; one which increases rather than decreases the capacity of the disinherited to participate with power in all of the structures of our common life. Without this capacity to *participate with power*—i.e., to have some organized political and economic strength to really influence people with whom one interacts— integration is not meaningful. For the issue is not one of racial balance but of honest interracial interaction.

For this kind of interaction to take place, all people need power, whether black or white. We regard as sheer hypocrisy or as a blind and dangerous illusion the view that opposes love to power. Love should be a controlling element in power, not power itself. So long as white churchmen continue to moralize and misinterpret Christian love, so long will justice continue to be subverted in this land.

III. To Negro Citizens: Power and Justice

Both the anguished cry for "black power" and the confused emotional response to it can be understood if the whole controversy is put in the context of American history. Especially must we understand the irony involved in the pride of Americans regarding their ability to act as individuals on the one hand, and their tendency to act as members of ethnic groups on the other hand. In the tensions of this part of our history is revealed both the tragedy and the hope of human redemption in America.

America has asked its Negro citizens to fight for opportunity *as individuals* whereas at certain points in our history what we have needed most has been opportunity for the whole group, not just for selected and approved Negroes. Thus in 1863, the slaves were made legally free, as individuals, but the real question regarding personal and group power to maintain that freedom was pushed aside. Power at that time for a mainly rural people meant land and tools to work the land. In the words of Thaddeus Stevens, power meant "40 acres and a mule." But this power was not made available to the slaves and we see the results today in the pushing of a landless peasantry off the farms into big cities where they come in search mainly of the power to be free. What they find are only the formalities of unenforced legal freedom. So we must ask, "What is the nature of the power which we seek and need today?" Power today is essentially organizational power. It is not a thing lying about in the streets to be fought over. It is a thing which, in some measure, already belongs to Negroes and which must be developed by Negroes in

relationship with the great resources of this nation.

Getting power necessarily involves reconciliation. We must first be reconciled to ourselves lest we fail to recognize the resources we already have and upon which we can build. We must be reconciled to ourselves as persons and to ourselves as an historical group. This means we must find our way to a new self-image in which we can feel a normal sense of pride in self, including our variety of skin color and the manifold textures of our hair. As long as we are filled with hatred for ourselves we will be unable to respect others.

At the same time, if we are seriously concerned about power then we must build upon that which we already have. "Black power" is already present to some extent in the Negro church, in Negro fraternities and sororities, in our professional associations, and in the opportunities afforded to Negroes who make decisions in some of the integrated organizations of our society.

We understand the reasons by which these limited forms of "black power" have been rejected by some of our people. Too often the Negro church has stirred its members away from the reign of God in *this world* to a distorted and complacent view of *an otherworldly* conception of God's power. We commit ourselves as churchmen to make more meaningful in the life of our institution our conviction that Jesus Christ reigns in the "here" and "now" as well as in the future he brings in upon us. We shall, therefore, use more of the resources of our churches in working for human justice in the places of social change and upheaval where our Master is already at work.

At the same time, we would urge that Negro social and professional organizations develop new roles for engaging the problem of equal opportunity and put less time into the frivolity of idle chatter and social waste.

We must not apologize for the existence of this form of group power, for we have been oppressed as a group, not as individuals. We will not find our way out of that oppression until both we and America accept the need for Negro Americans as well as for Jews, Italians, Poles and white Anglo-Saxon Protestants, among others, to have and to wield group power.

However, if power is sought merely as an end in itself, it tends to turn upon those who seek it. Negroes need power in order to participate more effectively at all levels of the life of our nation. We are glad that none of those civil rights leaders who have asked for "black power" have suggested that it means a new form of isolationism or a foolish effort at domination. But we must be clear about why we need to be reconciled with the white majority. It is *not* because we are only one-tenth of the population in America; for we do not need to be reminded of the awesome power wielded by the 90% majority. We see and feel that power every day in the destructions heaped upon our families and upon the nation's cities. We do not need to be threatened by such cold and heartless statements. For we are men, not children, and we are growing out of our fear of that power, which can hardly hurt us any more in the future than it does in the present or has in the past. Moreover, those bare figures conceal the potential political strength which is ours if we organize properly in the big cities and establish effective alliances.

Neither must we rest our concern for reconciliation with our white brothers on the fear that failure to do so would damage gains already made by the civil rights movement. If those gains are in fact real, they will withstand the claims of our people for power and justice, not just for a few select Negroes here and there, but for the masses of our citizens. We must rather rest our concern for reconciliation on the firm ground that we and all other Americans *are* one. Our history and destiny are indissolubly linked. If the future is to belong to any of us, it must be prepared for all of us whatever our racial or religious background. For in the final analysis, we are *persons* and the power of all groups must be wielded to make visible our common humanity.

The future of America will belong to neither white nor black unless all Americans work together at the task of rebuilding our cities. We must organize not only among ourselves but with other groups in order that we can, together, gain power sufficient to change this nation's sense of what is *now* important and what must be done *now*. We must work with the remainder of the nation to organize whole cities for the task of making the rebuilding of our cities first priority in the use of our resources. This is more important than who gets to the moon first or the war in Vietnam.

To accomplish this task we cannot expend our energies in spastic or ill-tempered explosions without meaningful goals. We must move from the politics of philanthropy to the politics of metropolitan development for equal opportunity. We must relate all groups of the city together in new ways in order that the truth of our cities might be laid bare and in order that, together, we can lay claim to the great resources of our nation to make truth more human.

*IV. To the Mass Media:
     Power and Truth*

The ability or inability of all people in America to understand the upheavals of our day depends greatly on the way power and truth operate in the mass media. During the Southern demonstrations for civil rights, you men of the communications industry performed an invaluable service for the entire country by revealing plainly to all ears and eyes, the ugly truth of a brutalizing system of overt discrimination and segregation. Many of you were mauled and injured, and it took courage for you to stick with the task. You were instruments of change and not merely purveyors of unrelated facts. You were able to do this by dint of personal courage and by reason of the power of national news agencies which supported you.

Today, however, your task and ours is more difficult. The truth that needs revealing today is not so clear-cut in its outlines, nor is there a national consensus to help you form relevant points of view. Therefore, nothing is now more important than that you look for a variety of sources of truth in order that the limited perspectives of all of us might be corrected. Just as you related to a broad spectrum of people in Mississippi instead of relying only on police records and establishment figures, so must you operate in New York City, Chicago and Cleveland.

The power to support you in this endeavor *is present* in our country. It must be searched out. We desire to use our limited influence to help relate you to the variety of experience in the Negro community so that limited controversies are not blown up into the final truth about us. The fate of this country is, to no small extent, dependent upon how you interpret the crises upon us, so that human truth is disclosed and human needs are met.

Signatories:

Bishop John D. Bright, Sr., AME Church, First Episcopal District, Philadelphia, Pennsylvania

The Rev. John Bryan, Connecticut Council of Churches, Hartford, Connecticut

Suffragan Bishop John M. Burgess, The Episcopal Church, Boston, Massachusetts

The Rev. W. Sterling Cary, Grace Congregational Church, New York, N.Y.

The Rev. Charles E. Cobb, St. John Church (UCC), Springfield, Mass.

The Rev. Caesar D. Coleman, Christian Methodist Episcopal Church, Memphis, Tennessee

The Rev. Joseph C. Coles, Williams Institutional CME Church, New York, New York

The Rev. George A. Crawley, Jr., St. Paul Baptist Church, Baltimore, Maryland

The Rev. O. Herbert Edwards, Trinity Baptist Church, Baltimore, Md.

The Rev. Bryant George, United Presbyterian Church in the U.S.A., New York, New York

Bishop Charles F. Golden, The Methodist Church, Nashville, Tenn.

The Rev. Quinland R. Gordon, The Episcopal Church, New York, N.Y.

The Rev. James Hargett, Church of Christian Fellowship, U.C.C., Los Angeles, Calif.

The Rev. Edler Hawkins, St. Augustine Presbyterian Church, New York, New York

The Rev. Reginald Hawkins, United Presbyterian Church, Charlotte, North Carolina

Dr. Anna Arnold Hedgeman, Commission on Religion and Race, National Council of Churches, New York, New York

The Rev. R. E. Hodd, Gary, Indiana

The Rev. H. R. Hughes, Bethel, A.M.E. Church, New York, N.Y.

The Rev. Kenneth Hughes, St. Bartholomew's Episcopal Church, Cambridge, Massachusetts

The Rev. Donald G. Jacobs, St. James A.M.E. Church, Cleveland, Ohio

The Rev. J. L. Joiner, Emanual A.M.E. Church, New York, New York

The Rev. Arthur A. Jones, Metropolitan A.M.E. Church, Philadelphia, Pennsylvania

The Rev. Stanley King, Sabathini Baptist Church, Minneapolis, Minnesota

The Rev. Earl Wesley Lawson, Emanual Baptist Church, Malden, Mass.

The Rev. David Licorish, Abyssinian Baptist Church, New York, N.Y.

The Rev. Arthur B. Mack, St. Thomas A.M.E.Z. Church, Haverstraw, N.Y.

The Rev. James W. Mack, South United Church of Christ, Chicago, Ill.

The Rev. O. Clay Maxwell, Jr., Baptist Ministers Conference of New York City and Vicinity, New York, New York.

The Rev. Leon Modeste, the Episcopal Church, New York, New York

Bishop Noah W. Moore, Jr., The Methodist
 Church, Southwestern Area, Houston, Texas
The Rev. David Nickerson, Episcopal Society
 for Cultural and Racial Unity, Atlanta, Georgia
The Rev. LeRoy Patrick, Bethesda United Pres-
 byterian Church, Pittsburgh, Pennsylvania
The Rev. Benjamin F. Payton, Commission on
 Religion and Race, National Council of
 Churches, New York, New York
The Rev. Isaiah P. Pogue, St. Mark's Presbyter-
 ian Church, Cleveland, Ohio
The Rev. Sandy F. Ray, Empire Baptist State
 Convention, Brooklyn, N.Y.
Bishop Herbert B. Shaw, Presiding Bishop,
 Third Episcopal District, A.M.E.Z. Church,
 Wilmington, N.C.
The Rev. Stephen P. Spottswood, Commission
 on Race and Cultural Relations, Detroit
 Council of Churches, Detroit, Michigan
The Rev. Henri A. Stines, Church of the
 Atonement, Washington, D.C.
Bishop James S. Thomas, Resident Bishop, Iowa
 Area, The Methodist Church, Des Moines, Iowa

The Rev. V. Simpson Turner, Mt. Carmel Bap-
 tist Church, Brooklyn, N.Y.
The Rev. Edgar Ward, Grace Presbyterian
 Church, Chicago, Ill.
The Rev. Paul M. Washington, Church of the
 Advocate, Philadelphia, Pa.
The Rev. Frank L. Williams, Methodist Church,
 Baltimore, Maryland
The Rev. John W. Williams, St. Stephen's
 Baptist Church, Kansas City, Mo.
The Rev. Gayraud Wilmore, United Presby-
 terian Church U.S.A., New York, New York
The Rev. M. L. Wilson, Covenant Baptist
 Church, New York, New York
The Rev. Robert H. Wilson, Corresponding
 Secretary, National Baptist Convention of
 America, Dallas, Texas
The Rev. Nathan Wright, Episcopal Diocese of
 Newark, Newark. N.J.

(Organizational affiliation given for identification purposes only.)

APPENDIX B

RACISM AND THE ELECTIONS

THE AMERICAN DILEMMA: 1966

Advertisement which appeared in
The New York Times, *Sunday, November 6, 1966*

Issued November 3, 1966
at the Statue of Liberty by the
National Committee of Negro Churchmen
    A few days ago the 80th anniversary of
the Statue of Liberty was celebrated here
on Liberty Island. On November 8, a so-
called "white backlash" will confront the
American people with a fateful choice in
the elections across the country. We, an
informal group of Negro churchmen,
assembled from the four corners of this
land, gather here today in order to high-
light the critical moral issues which confront the American people in those
elections—issues symbolized here in the
Statue of Liberty.

    Our purpose here is neither to beg nor
to borrow, but to state the determination
of black men in America to exact from
this nation not one whit less than our full
manhood rights. We will not be cowed
nor intimidated in the land of our birth.
We intend that the truth of this country,
as experienced by black men, will be
heard. We shall state this truth from the
perspective of the Christian faith and in
the light of our experience with the Lord
of us all, in the bleakness of this racially
idolatrous land.
    The inscription inside the Statue of
Liberty, entitled "The New Colossus,"

refers to America as the "Mother of Exiles." It concludes with these moving words:

"Keep ancient land, your storied
   pomp!" cries she
With silent lips. "Give me your tired,
   your poor,
Your huddled masses yearning to
   breathe free.
The wretched refuse of your teeming
   shore.
Send these, the homeless, tempest-tost
   to me.
I lift my lamp beside the Golden Door!"

This poem focuses on the linked problems of identity and power which have been so tragically played out on the stage of this nation's history. "Mother of Exiles" and "The New Colossus"—these symbols capture both the variety of groups and experience out of which this nation has been hammered and the fervent hope of many early Americans that in this land the world would see a new and more human use of power, dedicated to the proposition that all men are created equal.

We remind Americans that in our beginnings we were all exiles, strangers sojourning in an unfamiliar land. Even the first black men who set foot on these shores came, as did most white men, in the role of pilgrims, not as slaves. Sharing common aspirations and hopes for a land where freedom could take root and live, for the briefest of moments black men and white men found each other in a community of trust and mutual acceptance.

However, if America became a "Mother of Exiles" for white men she became at the same time a cruel system of bondage and inhumanity to black men. Far from finding here a maternal acceptance, her black sons were thrust into the depth of despair, at times so hopeless that it wrung from their lips the sorrow song: "Sometimes I feel like a motherless child." What anguish is keener, what rejection more complete, or what alienation more poignant than this experience which called forth the metaphor, "motherless child"?

But that is only part of our story. For somewhere in the depth of their experience within this great land, those same black men and women found a ground of faith and hope on which to stand. Never accepting on the inside the identity forced upon them by a brutalizing white power, they also sang—even prior to emancipation—"Before I'll be a slave, I'll be buried in my grave and go home to my Lord and be free." A faith of this quality and integrity remains alive today.

There is, to be sure, a continuing dilemma of "crisis and commitment" in our country. But it is not the quarrels among the civil rights leaders, nor is it the debate about Black Power, nor is it the controversy surrounding the riots in our cities. The crisis is what it has always been since shortly after the first black Americans set foot upon these shores. It is not a crisis rooted in the Negro community. It is a "crisis of commitment" among white Americans who have consistently taken two steps forward toward becoming mature men on race and one and a half steps backward at the same time. The power of "The New Colossus" has never been fully committed to eliminating this monstrous racism from the life of the American people.

Look at the record of fitful and mincing steps forward and of cowardly steps away from the goal of racial justice. The slaves were freed in 1863, but the nation refused to give them land to make that emancipation meaningful. Simultaneously, the nation was giving away millions of acres in the midwest and west—a gift marked "for whites only." Thus an economic floor was placed under the new peasants from Europe but America's oldest peasantry was provided only an abstract freedom. In the words of Frederick Douglass, emancipation made the slaves "free to hunger; free to the winter and rains of heaven . . . free without roofs to cover them or bread to eat or land to cultivate. . . . We gave them freedom and famine at the same time. The marvel is that they still live."

We should, therefore, be neither shocked nor surprised that our slums today confront us with the bitter fruits of that ancient theft. Is it conceivable that the shrill cry "Burn, Baby, Burn" in Watts, Los Angeles, and across this country, could ever be invented by men with reasonable chances to make a living, to live in a decent neighborhood, to get an adequate education for their children? Is it conceivable that men with reasonable prospects for life, liberty and the pursuit of happiness for themselves and for their children could ever put the torch to their own main streets? The answer is obvious. These are the anguished, desperate acts of men, women and children who have been taught to hate themselves and who have been herded and confined like cattle in rat-infested slums.

Frederick Douglass is indeed correct when he suggests that "the marvel is that Negroes are still alive" not to mention sane. Look at the record. We submit that to pass a Civil Rights Bill as this nation did in 1875 and then refuse to enforce it; to pass another Civil Rights Bill (weaker this time) in 1964 and then refuse to enforce it; to begin an anti-poverty program with insufficient funds in the first place and then to put the lion's share of this miniscule budget into Head Start programs when unemployment among Negro men continues to sky-rocket; to declare segregation in our schools unconstitutional as the Supreme Court did in 1954, and then refuse to end it forthwith; to set up guidelines for desegregating hospitals and then refuse to appropriate moneys for the enforcement of these guidelines; to insist on civil rights legislation aimed at the south and then to defeat the first piece of such legislation relevant to areas outside the south; to preach "law and order" into the anguish of Negro slums in full view of the contributions of policemen to that anguish and then to insist that policemen be their own judges; to hear suburban politicians declaim against open occupancy in one breath and in the very next breath insist that they are not racists: these are the ironies which stare us in the face and make it all but impossible to talk about how much "progress" has been made. The fact of the matter is if black Americans are not accorded basic human and constitutional rights which white Americans gain immediately upon their entry into citizenship, then there really are no substantive gains of which to speak.

Therefore, we will not be intimidated by the so-called "white backlash," for white America has been "backlashing" on the fundamental human and constitutional rights of Negro Americans since the 18th century. The election of racists in November will merely be a continuation of this pattern.

But: Let us try to be very clear about one thing, America. Black Americans are determined to have all of their full human and constitutional rights. We will not cease to agitate this issue with every means available to men of faith and dignity until justice is done.

We are dealing at bottom with a question of relationship between black and white, between rich and poor, ultimately between believers in different gods. We support all of our civil rights leaders for we believe that they all have important insights to share with us on this critical question. For our part, we submit that our basic goal in this struggle is to make it possible for all persons and groups to participate with power at all levels of our society. Integration is not an aesthetic goal designed to add token bits of color to institutions controlled entirely by whites. Integration is a political goal with the objective of making it possible for Negroes and other Americans to express the vitality of their personal and group life in institutions which fundamentally belong to all Americans.

If the tremendous power of this nation —this "New Colossus"—begins to move "with conquering limbs astride from land to land," then we are bound to forget the tired, the poor, the "huddled masses yearning to be free." America is rich and powerful. But America is neither infinitely rich nor omnipotent. Even America must make choices.

We submit that the resolution of the crises which is upon us requires a change in the nation's priorities. The welfare and dignity of all Americans is more important than the priorities being given to military expansion, space exploration or the production of supersonic jet airliners.

To this end, we of the Negro church call for a massive mobilization of the resources in the Negro community in order to give leadership in the fulfillment not only of our own destiny but in order to help produce a more sane white America.

We further call upon white churchmen to join us by endeavoring to mobilize the resources of the white community in completing with us the task at hand.

Finally, we say to the American people, white and black, there is no turning back of the clock of time. America cannot be

America by electing "white backlash" candidates in the November elections.

Again we say: America is at the cross-road. Either we become the democracy we can become, or we tread the path to self-destruction.

NATIONAL COMMITTEE OF
NEGRO CHURCHMEN
Room 552, 475 Riverside Drive
New York, N.Y. 10027

The Rev. William Aaron, The Congregational Church of God, New York, N.Y.

Bishop G. Wayman Blakely, 16th Episcopal District, A.M.E. Church, Philadelphia, Pa.

Bishop John D. Bright, Sr., A.M.E. Church, First Episcopal District, Philadelphia, Pa.

The Rev. John Bryan, Connecticut Council of Churches, Hartford, Conn.

Suffragan Bishop John M. Burgess, The Episcopal Church, Boston, Mass.

The Rev. W. Sterling Cary, Grace Congregational Church, New York. N.Y.

The Rev. Tollie L. Caution, Sr., Episcopal Church Center, New York, N.Y.

The Rev. Charles E. Cobb, Committee for Racial Justice Now, United Church of Christ, New York, N.Y.

The Rev. Caesar D. Coleman, Christian Methodist Episcopal Church, Memphis, Tenn.

The Rev. Joseph C. Coles, Williams Institutional C.M.E. Church, New York, N.Y.

The Rev. George A. Crawley, Jr., St. Paul Baptist Church, Baltimore, Md.

The Rev. Walter D. Dennis, Cathedral of St. John the Divine, New York, N.Y.

The Rev. O. Herbert Edwards, Trinity Baptist Church, Baltimore, Md.

The Rev. Bryant George, United Presbyterian Church in the U.S.A., New York, N.Y.

Bishop Charles F. Golden, The Methodist Church, Nashville, Tenn.

The Rev. Quinland R. Gordon, The Episcopal Church, New York, N.Y.

The Rev. Nathaniel T. Grady, Sr., Moore Memorial A.M.E. Zion Church, Bronx, N.Y.

The Rev. James Hargett, Church of Christian Fellowship, U.C.C., Los Angeles, Calif.

The Rev. Earl H. Harrison. Shiloh Baptist Church, Washington, D.C.

The Rev. Edler Hawkins, St. Augustine Presbyterian Church, New York, N.Y.

The Rev. Reginald Hawkins, United Presbyterian Church, Charlotte, N.C.

Dr. Anna Arnold Hedgeman, Commission on Religion and Race, National Council of Churches, New York, N.Y.

The Rev. J. Clinton Haggard, Board of Foreign Missions, A.M.E. Zion Church, New York, N.Y.

The Rev. Bernard Holliday, Manhattan Division, Protestant Council, New York, N.Y.

The Rev. R. E. Hood, Gary, Ind.

The Rev. H. R. Hughes, Bethel A.M.E. Church, New York, N.Y.

The Rev. Kenneth Hughes, St. Bartholomew's Episcopal Church, Cambridge, Mass.

The Rev. Donald G. Jacobs, St. James A.M.E. Church, Cleveland, Ohio

The Rev. J. L. Joiner, Emanuel A.M.E. Church, New York, N.Y.

The Rev. Arthur A. Jones, Metropolitan A.M.E. Church, Philadelphia, Pa.

The Rev. D. E. King, Friendship Baptist Church, New York, N.Y.

The Rev. Stanley King, Sabathini Baptist Church, Minneapolis, Minn.

The Rev. Earl Wesley Lawson, Emanuel Baptist Church, Malden, Mass.

The Rev. J. Oscar Lee, Div. of Christian Life and Mission, Nat'l Council of Churches, New York, N.Y.

The Rev. David Licorish, Abyssinian Baptist Church, New York, N.Y.

The Rev. Arthur B. Mack, St. Thomas A.M.E. Zion Church, Haverstraw, N.Y.

The Rev. James W. Mack, South United Church of Christ, Chicago, Ill.

Robert W. Mance, M.D., Secretary of Finance, A.M.E. Church, Washington, D.C.

The Rev. O. Clay Maxwell, Jr., Baptist Ministers Conference of New York City and Vicinity, New York, N.Y.

The Rev. Leon Modeste, The Episcopal Church, New York, N.Y.

Bishop Noah W. Moore, Jr., The Methodist Church, Southwestern Area, Houston, Tex.

The Rev. David Nickerson, Episcopal Society for Cultural and Racial Unity, Atlanta, Ga.

The Rev. LeRoy Patrick, Bethesda United Presbyterian Church, Pittsburgh, Pa.

The Rev. Arthur J. Payne, Enon Baptist Church, Baltimore, Md.

The Rev. Benjamin F. Payton, Commission on Religion and Race, National Council of Churches, New York, N.Y.

The Rev. Channing E. Phillips, Lincoln Temple, United Church of Christ, Washington, D.C.

The Rev. Isaiah P. Pogue, St. Mark's Presbyterian Church, Cleveland, O.

The Rev. Sandy F. Ray, President, Empire Baptist State Convention, Brooklyn, N.Y.

The Rev. H. P. Sharper, Abyssinian Baptist Church, Newark, N.J.

Bishop Herbert B. Shaw, Presiding Bishop, Third Episcopal District, A.M.E. Zion Church, Wilmington, N.C.

The Rev. Stephen P. Spottswood, Commission on Race and Cultural Relations, Detroit Council of Churches, Detroit, Mich.

The Rev. Henri A. Stines, Church of the Atonement, Washington, D.C.

The Rev. Richard R. Stokes, President, A.M.E. Minister's Alliance of Greater New York

The Rev. Gardner C. Taylor, President, Progressive National Baptist Convention, Inc., New York, N.Y.

Bishop James Thomas, Resident Bishop, Iowa Area, The Methodist Church, Des Moines, Iowa

The Rev. Paul F. Thurston, President, A.M.E. Zion Ministers' Alliance of New York and vicinity

The Rev. V. Simpson Turner, Mt. Carmel Baptist Church, Brooklyn, N.Y.

The Rev. Edgar Ward, Grace Presbyterian Church, Chicago, Ill.

The Rev. Paul M. Washington, Church of the Advocate, Philadelphia, Pa.

The Rev. U. B. Whitfield, President, Baptist Ministers Conference of Greater New York, New York, N.Y.

The Rev. Frank L. Williams, Metropolitan Methodist Church, Baltimore, Md.

The Rev. John W. Williams, St. Stephen's Baptist Church, Kansas City, Mo.

The Rev. Gayraud Wilmore, United Presbyterian Church U.S.A., New York, N.Y.

The Rev. M. L. Wilson, Convent Avenue Baptist Church, New York, N.Y.

The Rev. Nathan Wright, Episcopal Diocese of Newark, Newark, N.J.

The Rev. Leslie R. Agent, Cornerstone Baptist Church, Brooklyn, N.Y.

Bishop George W. Baber, A.M.E. Church, Washington, D.C.

The Rev. Jack S. Bailey, Presbyterian Parish, Atlantic City, N.J.

The Rev. James K. Baldwin, St. James A.M.E. Church, Atlantic City, N.J.

The Rev. Joseph B. Bethea, Dist. Supt., The Methodist Church, Richmond, Va.

The Rev. Clayborne W. Black, New Shiloh Baptist Church, Baltimore, Md.

The Rev. Eustace L. Blake, Jones Tabernacle A.M.E. Church, Philadelphia, Pa.

The Rev. Walter D. Bowen, Tioga Presbyterian Church, Philadelphia, Pa.

The Rev. James P. Breeden, Commission on Religion and Race, National Council of Churches, New York, N.Y.

The Rev. H. B. Brightman, Presiding Elder, Atlantic City District, A.M.E. Church, Neptune, N.J.

The Rev. N. J. Brockman, Union Baptist Church, Greenville, S.C.

The Rev. Ralph E. Brower, St. Michael Methodist Church, Jersey City, N.J.

The Rev. C. Wellington Butts, Bethany Presbyterian Church, Englewood, N.J.

The Rev. Vernon R. Byrd, A.M.E. Church, Philadelphia, Pa.

The Rev. Henry Cade, Central Presbyterian Church, Newark, N.J.

The Rev. Gilbert H. Caldwell, Union Methodist Church, Boston, Mass.

The Rev. Clarence L. Cave, United Presbyterian Board of Christian Education, Philadelphia, Pa.

The Rev. Frank E. Churchill, Hood Memorial A.M.E. Zion Church, New York, N.Y.

The Rev. C. H. Churn, Union Temple Baptist Church, Baltimore, Md.

The Rev. Harold A. L. Clement, Varick Memorial A.M.E. Zion Church, New Haven, Conn.

The Rev. Junius W. Cofield, Star of Bethlehem Baptist Church, Ossining, N.Y.

The Rev. R. W. Coleman, Mt. Zion A.M.E. Church, Dover, Del.

The Rev. John W. P. Collier, Jr., A.M.E. Union Church, Philadelphia, Pa.

The Rev. D. A. Cowart, Mt. Pisgah A.M.E. Church, Washington, N.J.

The Rev. Jeffrey L. Cuffee, St. Augustine's Chapel, Trinity Parish, New York, N.Y.

The Rev. A. K. David, Macedonia A.M.E. Church, Flushing, N.Y.

The Rev. Henri Deas, Newman Memorial Methodist Church, Brooklyn, N.Y.

The Rev. Henry R. Delaney, Israel Metropolitan C.M.E. Church, Washington, D.C.

The Rev. Billie E. Dukes, South Congregational Church, Brooklyn, N.Y.

The Rev. David R. Dunlap, Woodlawn Methodist Church, Alexandria, Va.

The Rev. Edwin R. Edmonds, Dixwell Avenue Congregational Church, New Haven, Conn.

The Rev. Charles H. Foggie, Wesley Center A.M.E. Zion Church, Pittsburgh, Pa.

The Rev. William K. Fox, Assistant General Secretary, New Jersey Council of Churches, East Orange, N.J.

The Rev. Kenneth E. Frazier, Calloway Methodist Church, Arlington, Va.

The Rev. J. Isaiah Goodman, First Baptist Church, Englewood, N.J.

The Rev. C. E. Grogan, First Calvary Baptist Church, New York, N.Y.

The Rev. David E. Hackett, St. Paul's A.M.E. Church, New Haven, Conn.

The Rev. Arthur L. Hardge, Hood Memorial A.M.E. Zion Church, Providence, R.I.

The Rev. John J. Hicks, St. Mark's Methodist Church, New York, N.Y.

The Rev. Richard Allen Hildebrand, Bridge Street A.M.E. Church, Brooklyn, N.Y.

The Rev. Charles E. Houston, Shiloh Baptist Church, Tuckahoe, N.Y.

The Rev. O. Ureille Ifill, Sr., St. James A.M.E. Church, Chambersburg, Pa.

The Rev. J. J. Jackson, Mount Pisgah A.M.E. Church, Jersey City, N.J.

The Rev. Solomon N. Jacobs, St. Andrew's Episcopal Church, Cleveland, Ohio

The Rev. John H. Johnson, Jr., Presiding Elder, A.M.E. Church, Mt. Holly, N.J.

The Rev. James Arthur Jones, Halsey Temple C.M.E. Church, Philadelphia, Pa.

The Rev. James E. Jones, Westminster Presbyterian Church, Los Angeles, Cal.

The Rev. Leroy Judge, St. John's A.M.E. Church, New York, N.Y.

The Rev. A. R. Kelley, Sr., The Greater Calvary Baptist Church, West Atco, N.J.

The Rev. Thomas Kilgore, Jr., Second Baptist Church, Los Angeles, Cal.

The Rev. A. R. Lloyd, Star Baptist Church, Corona, N.Y.

The Rev. George L. Lloyd, Fourth Moravian Church, New York, N.Y.

The Rev. Irvin C. Lockman, Mt. Calvary Methodist Church, New York, N.Y.

The Rev. Andrew Wesley Mapp, Metropolitan A.M.E. Zion Church, Jersey City, N.J.

The Rev. Calvin B. Marshall, Park Street A.M.E. Zion Church, Peekskill, N.Y.

The Rev. George E. Martin, Jr., First Baptist Church, Riverhead, N.Y.

The Rev. Baxter L. Matthews, Union Baptist Church, Baltimore, Md.

The Rev. Joseph H. May, Mt. Carmel Baptist Church, Brooklyn, N.Y.

The Rev. C. Lincoln McGee, Trinity United Presbyterian Church, Montclair, N.J.

The Rev. Joseph McKenzie, Bethel A.M.E. Church, Setauket, N.Y.

The Rev. G. W. McMurray, Mother A.M.E. Zion Church, New York, N.Y.

The Rev. Donald G. Ming, Allen A.M.E. Church, Jamaica, N.Y.

The Rev. Paul J. Morrison, Trinity A.M.E. Church, Corona, N.Y.

The Rev. Arnold D. Nearn, Presiding Elder, A.M.E. Church, Philadelphia, Pa.

The Rev. Samuel E. Nesmith, Roberts Memorial Methodist Church, Alexandria, Va.

The Rev. John H. Nichols, First Calvary Baptist Church, Brooklyn, N.Y.

The Rev. Roy Nichols, Salem Methodist Church, New York, N.Y.

The Rev. D. M. Owens, St. James A.M.E. Church, Newark, N.J.

The Rev. Arthur W. Parker, New York, N.Y.

The Rev. E. B. Phillips, Greater Galilee Baptist Church, Milwaukee, Wis.

The Rev. Otis O. Pickett, Lowndes Hill Baptist Church, Greenville, S.C.

The Rev. R. L. Pruitt, Metropolitan A.M.E. Church, New York, N.Y.

The Rev. J. G. Ragin, Mt. Zion A.M.E. Church, New York, N.Y.

The Rev. Logan Rearse, Cornerstone Baptist Church of Christ, Baltimore, Md.

The Rev. E. P. Reese, New Ebenezer Baptist Church, New York, N.Y.

The Rev. Edward M. Revels, St. Paul Christian Community Church, Baltimore, Md.

The Rev. J. Metz Rollins, Jr., United Presbyterian Church, New York, N.Y.

The Rev. Warner H. Sanford, Dixwell Avenue Congregational Church, New Haven, Conn.

The Rev. R. L. Saunders, National Christian Missionary Convention, Brooklyn, N.Y.

The Rev. Horace Sharper, Abyssinian Baptist Church, Newark, N.J.

The Rev. A. J. Simmons, Bethel A.M.E. Church, Lancaster, Pa.

The Rev. G. T. Sims, Sr., Allen A.M.E. Church, Newark, N.J.

The Rev. E. C. Smith, Metropolitan Baptist Church, Washington, D.C.

The Rev. James E. Smith, Gethsemane Baptist Church and General Baptist State Convention of New York

The Rev. Oswald G. Smith, Mt. Zion Baptist Church, Arlington, Va.

The Rev. R. L. Speaks, First A.M.E. Zion Church, Brooklyn, N.Y.

The Rev. Harold Speights, St. Paul A.M.E. Church, Kenilworth, N.J.

The Rev. Joseph E. Taylor, Israel Metropolitan C.M.E. Church, Washington, D.C.

The Rev. L. E. Terrell, Union Baptist Church, New York, N.Y.

The Rev. Harold A. Thomas, Witherspoon Street Presbyterian Church, Princeton, N.J.

The Rev. Jesse G. Truvillion, Lafayette Presbyterian Church, Jersey City, N.J.

The Rev. Eugene Turner, United Presbyterian Church, Philadelphia, Pa.

The Rev. Irvin W. Underhill, First United Presbyterian Church, Nunda, N.Y.

The Rev. Sam H. Wesley Varner, St. John's Lutheran Church, Bronx, N.Y.

The Rev. Shelton Waters, First African Presbyterian Church, Philadelphia, Pa.

The Rev. Leon W. Watts, Presbytery of New York City, New York, N.Y.

The Rev. Leamon W. White, Bethel Baptist Church, Washington, D.C.

The Rev. Alphonso Whitfield, Hope Chapel A.M.E. Zion Church, Utica, N.Y.

The Rev. Andrew E. Whitted, St. Catherine A.M.E. Zion Church, New Rochelle, N.Y.

The Rev. A. Lewis Williams, Bethel A.M.E. Church, Morristown, N.J.

The Rev. Edward C. Williams, United Presbyterian Church, New York, N.Y.

The Rev. Voluton H. Williams, Trinity C.M.E. Church, Brooklyn, N.Y.

The Rev. W. N. Williams, Brown's Temple C.M.E. Church, Asheville, N.C.

The Rev. William T. Williams, Mother A.M.E. Zion Church, New York, N.Y.

The Rev. Bruce P. Williamson, St. Mary's Episcopal Church, Philadelphia, Pa.

The Rev. Lorentho Wooden, St. Simon's Episcopal Church, New Rochelle, N.Y.

The Rev. John W. Wright, Bethesda Baptist Church, Jersey City, N.J.

The Rev. Ward D. Yerby, Perkins Square Baptist Church, Baltimore, Md.

THE CHURCH AND THE URBAN CRISIS*

A Preamble to Statements Developed at the
National Council of Churches
Conference on the Church and Urban Tensions
Washington, D.C., Sept. 27–30, 1967†

More than 100 persons from seventeen denominations met in Washington, under the auspices of the National Council of Churches, from September 27 to 30.

We came together from all over the nation, after a summer of anguish and revolt, expectantly and fearfully.

We came in an hour of grave crisis in the cities of our country—a crisis of severe distrust and alienation between black and white both within and outside of the churches.

We came to wrestle once again with the problem of our disorder and disobedience as Christians and God's design for renewal and reconciliation in a time of world-wide revolution.

We came conscious of the context in which any meaningful conversation about church strategy for racial justice could take place among us. The context of Black Power—that mood and strategy of the black community which is transforming the civil rights movement into a movement for the identity, self-image and dignity of black people through the development of legitimate power in the arenas of political social and economic decision-making in the United States.

The overarching question of our discussions was "Who really are we who seek in our various places to bear witness to the God of justice and reconciliation between white Americans and black Americans?" To put the matter another way, we were forced in Washington to ask of ourselves, "What are we required to face honestly about ourselves—about our whiteness and our blackness—before we are able to confront the world together in the name of Jesus Christ, in whom we were made One?"

As we struggled with these questions, which really have to do with the existential nature of the Church in the United States, we came face to face with our own delusions and pretensions. We discovered that in order to learn the truth about ourselves and our situation, so successfully covered over by years of hypocrisy and dissimulation, we had to make a decision in ecumenical conferences under the aegis of the National Council. We made the decision to divide the conference into a white caucus and a black caucus.

Although we continued to meet together in plenary sessions, it was in these separate groups that some of us in Washington experienced more than ever before the scandal of our separateness in the two worlds and the two churches of America. We experienced also the most honest and intensive confrontation many of us have ever known with the tragic reality of American racism, the poverty of our own spirits and confessions and finally, the necessity of a strategic with-

*From the Department of Information, National Council of Churches, 475 Riverside Drive, New York, New York 10027.
†Document of the first "caucusizing" of a national ecumenical conference in the U.S.

drawal into our own separate staging-areas before we could emerge together to do battle with a common enemy on a common battlefield.

Out of the two caucuses of this conference came the two statements which are reproduced below. They are neither definitive nor are they conclusive positions for white and black churchmen. They do mark the beginning of what some of us believe is a new and more relevant dialogue about the role of the church in the urban crisis. They also suggest some of the themes and commitments that we who were together in Washington wish to explore further as we plan together and separately for participation in the racial revolution.

Without pretending that we have spoken either the ultimate or the authoritative word, we make bold to commend this document to churchmen for whatever study and implementation they, by conscience and conviction, are guided to make.

A DECLARATION OF BLACK CHURCHMEN

Statement Developed at the NCC Conference on the Church and Urban Tensions, Washington, D.C., Sept. 27–30, 1967

We, Black Churchmen, meeting in caucus find ourselves profoundly distressed, disturbed, frustrated and in a state of utter disquietude about a nature and mission of the church in a time of revolution. We have come to realize that Black Power is an expression of the need for Black Authenticity in a white-dominated society, a society which has from its earliest beginnings displayed unadulterated racism.

We affirm without fear of repudiation the meaningfulness of blackness and our identity as Black Churchmen. We confess the guilt which is ours for past actions and inaction in failing to be instruments for the expression of the will of God as Black Churchmen. We therefore propose now to speak and act, out of our own shame and guilt, concerning the lack of the Church's responsiveness to the needs of black people seeking to be free and human in a dehumanizing world.

White Churches

We call upon the white churches at this point in history to recognize that in spite of the many commendable contributions in the past to the struggle for social justice, we have come to a point when the very structures, forms and priorities are being seriously questioned particularly by the Black Power Revolution. Racial Justice can no longer be considered just another cause pursued by a few while the rest of the church does business as usual. Moreover, it cannot simply be a cause alongside of other causes—to be used as a ploy to justify the existence of the Church, but must become the number one priority as it is the number one problem of the nation.

Therefore, we commend the belated action taken by the General Board of the National Council of Churches of Christ in the U.S.A. in its resolution "The Crisis within the Nation," September 14, 1967, wherein it pledges ten percent of its unrestricted capital funds for development in the Black community and calls upon its member constituents, among other things, to make available its resources for development in the Black community. It specifically states that "funds be used for the development of programs in ghetto communities which are planned and directed by representatives of those communities for maximum benefit of the communities." We recognize that this is an initial step in the right direction and call for its immediate implementation.

We further call upon the white churches to commit themselves to the following:

(1) To join with us in affirming the legitimacy of the Black Power movement and to be open to the word that God is speaking to us through the issues it raises.

(2) To turn in their distress to the leadership of the Black Church recognizing the insights born out of a history of struggle against the exclusion and oppression of Black people in Church and Society; supporting the initiatives born of these insights; and seeking the guidance, collaboration and support of the Black Churches in the formulation and implementation of all church policies and programs.

(3) To declare a three-year moratorium on suburban new church development, and make the funds available from such work in people-centered ministries in the Black and White communities.

Black Churches

Historically the Black Church in America represented an authentic expression of Black Power. It grew out of the needs of Black People to glorify God and to affirm their own humanity; to find a sense of identity; to have something controlled by Black People; to form an institution whose express purpose would be to celebrate, preserve and enhance the integrity of Blackness under the lordship of Christ, to be responsive to the needs of Black People and responsible to them.

The historic step to separate from the White Church was the first clear call for Black Power.

However, we confess that in recent times we have not lived up to our heritage, for we have not celebrated, preserved and enhanced the integrity of Blackness. Rather we have fallen prey to the dominance of White Society and have allowed the truth, meaningfulness and authenticity of the Black Church to be defamed by our easy acceptance of its goals, objectives and criteria for success. Therefore, the Black Church has unwittingly become a tool for our oppression, providing an easy vehicle for escape from the harsh realities of our own existence. This of necessity makes it impossible for us to be instruments of liberation which is our calling as Christians and particularly Black Christians.

Since as Black Churchmen we find ourselves in the unenviable role of the oppressor, we are in real danger of losing our existence and our reason for being, if indeed we have not already lost them. We rejoice in the Black Power Movement which is not only the renewed hope for Black People, but gives the Black Church, once again its reason for existing. We call upon Black Churchmen everywhere to embrace the Black Power Movement, to divest itself of the traditional churchly functions and goals which do not respond to the needs of a downtrodden, oppressed and alienated people.

We further call upon the Black Church to commit itself to the following:

(1) To the establishment of freedom schools to offset the degradation and omission of a white-dominated public school system.

(2) To workshops fostering Black family solidarity.

(3) To training lay leadership in community organization and other relevant skills.

(4) To massive effort to support financially Black groups for self-determination.

(5) To the removal of all images which suggest that God is white.

Having spoken to the Black Church and the White Church, we now speak specifically to Black Churchmen in Black Churches or Non-Black Churches.

On July 26, 1966 a group of Black Churchmen met to form a new movement in American Christendom—the National Committee of Negro Churchmen. The major purpose of this group was to declare that at this juncture of history, under the impetus of the Black Power Movement, Black Churchmen needed to consolidate their energies and resources in a consciously Black organization for the purpose of enhancing the self-image, dignity and power of the Black Community in America.

We support the National Committee of Negro Churchmen. We call upon Black Churchmen of the Black Church and Black Churchmen of the Non-Black Churches to participate in it. We call for support of the national committee by the Black and Non-Black Churches.

Furthermore, we call upon the National Committee of Negro Churchmen to complete the process of organization by:

(1) The establishment of a national headquarters with a paid secretariat.

(2) To establish regional offices through which every black churchman can participate in the institutional and theological renewal of Black Religion enabling it to make its unique contribution to the universal church free from pernicious racism.

(3) To divest itself of internal partisan politics and ecclesiastical gamesmanship.

(4) To structure itself in such a way as to provide the kind of revolutionary impetus needed for these crucial times.

(5) To call for a conference of Black theologians to consider the theological implications of Black Power.

Finally we call upon Black Churchmen who find themselves in Non-Black Churches either to find ways of exercising a high degree of influence over structures of those churches or to return home to the black expression of religion. We further call upon the Black Churchmen in Black Churches to insure the return of the Black Church to an expression of its original reason for being.

A DECLARATION OF WHITE CHURCHMEN

Statement Developed at the NCC Conference on the Church and Urban Tensions, Washington, D.C., Sept. 27–30, 1967

The problem of race in America is centered in white America.

The white church is a racist church.

The American black man did not create the ghettoes of our sick cities. White America has enslaved him.

The American black, by and large, does not own the ghettoes. They are owned by white men.

However, American blacks will transform the ghettoes. Whites must seek a way to transform themselves, or we will constitute an *apartheid* society.

The body gathered in this caucus are determined to transform the white society. We are encouraged by the courage of the black American brother who has shown that he will create a new black society in America. Therefore, where it is possible, we will move together for the transformation of American society.

Where it is not possible to work together at present, we will work separately, knowing at the same time that our separate work with blacks and whites is our common task and work together.

THE THEOLOGICAL COMMISSION PROJECT

of The National Committee of Negro Churchmen

by Gayraud S. Wilmore
Chairman, Theological Commission
Fall 1968

I

Since its inception in 1966, the National Committee of Negro Churchmen has raised important theological issues which have provided the substance of a continuing controversy and dialogue, both within and outside of the organization. Some of these issues have been introduced by the very existence of NCNC. For example, some white Lutheran churchmen have asked whether or not the latent purpose of the National Committee was schismatic, contrary to the dominant spirit of the ecumenical movement today and corrupted by a serious distortion of the concept of the unity of the Body of Christ. Some black Baptist churchmen, on the other hand, have looked askance at the new organization because of what they suspected was an inherent propensity to further institutionalize black religion by directing it toward a radical secularization in the context of Black Power, and therefore challenging the traditional spirituality and churchmanship of the five major black denominations.

Other questions, both theological and ethical, have been raised in various statements and deliverances of the NCNC and in formal and informal discussions at the meetings of the membership and the Board of Directors. For example, from the beginning, the theological program of the Church of the Black Madonna in Detroit has been a constant challenge to NCNC members—especially that congregation's view of the relevancy of the New Testament and the color of the historical Christ. Since the escalation of riots in urban ghettoes and the implication of black churchmen in these "acts of rebellion" NCNC members—as well as others—have seriously asked whether or not a theology of violence were possible and how it should be articulated and implemented within the black Christian community.

While the first two years of the National Committee's existence has been largely administrative, dealing with the problems of recruiting members, raising funds and setting up a national office, it is nevertheless true that essentially theological questions related to the existence, the goals and strategy of the organization have always been close at hand. It was, of course, inevitable that a coming together of churchmen from diverse theological and ecclesiastical traditions would force the consideration of difficult whys and wherefores—the search for a theological base upon which to stand. But the fact that this group was formed in the hurricane eye of a black revolution unprecedented in American history and at a time when the credibility of the Christian faith was being severely tested in the black ghettoes of the nation, created an even more intense climate of inquiry and concern about theological and ideological foundations than may have been generated in calmer days when clergymen came together to form ministerial alliances for mutual edification and the propagation of the Gospel.

The result has been, as attested by the national secular and religious press, a rising crescendo of voices from both the pulpit and pew demanding that black churchmen reexamine their beliefs; that unless they begin to speak and act relevantly in the present crisis they must prepare to die; that unless they "do their thing" in some kind of symbolic and actual disengagement from the opprobrium of a white racist Christianity, they have no right to exist in the black community. A call to "come let us reason together" has gone out from a restive black church leadership and it is reechoed again and again wherever clergy and laity congregate across denominational lines. An evocative theological dialogue is now in process and it is clear that its object is not esoteric quibble about irrelevant pieties, but a sober reassessment of the ground upon which we stand—the search from a firmer footing, a "faith-lock," from which black Christians can carry on a life and death struggle against the principalities and powers, the rulers of this present darkness in America. The National Committee of Negro Churchmen, in its brief history, has played a significant part in stimulating and programming the lively conversation that has now been joined by white and black churchmen across the nation.

II

Three basic documents of the National Committee reflect the main thrust of the theological critique and commentary which has issued from the current movement of black churchmen toward unity and renewal. They are the "Black Power Statement" of July 31, 1966, first published as a full page ad in *The New York Times;* the first Report of the Theological Commission, adopted by the membership at the first National Convocation in Dallas, November 1-3, 1967; and the "Statement of the National Committee of Negro Churchmen on the Urban Mission in a Time of Crisis" which was drafted and adopted by the NCNC Board of Directors at its meeting in Chicago on March 3, 1968.

The 1966 "Black Power Statement" attempted to analyze the nature of power in relation to conscience and corruption. It pointed out the distortion of ethical perception when "white people are justified in getting what they want through the use of power, but . . . Negro Americans must, either by nature or by circumstances, make their appeal only through conscience."

It further clarified the relationship of power and love as the foundation of a just society and declared that "integration" in either the church or society without meaningful *participation with power* is both inauthentic and demeaning. The 1966 Statement took note that, "Too often the Negro Church has stirred its members away from the reign of God in *this* world to a distorted and complacent view of an *otherworldly* conception of God's power." It pledged black churches to work for justice in places of change and upheaval, "where our Master is already at work."

The Statement on Black Power was an eloquent theological and ethical pronouncement which served notice that a militant black church, acknowledging both Carmichael and the moderate civil rights leaders, existed in the ghetto and that in style and posture it differed from, and bore judgment upon, a diffident liberal church establishment that was wilting in the face of white counter pressure to the "long, hot summer" of 1966.

The Report of the Theological Commission in Dallas [1967] was drafted by a small group charged with bringing before the membership the main lines of theological inquiry which might, at some future time, provide the basis for theological consultations—both among black scholars and theologians and between them and their white counterparts. Further, it was assumed in Dallas that some kind of "Barmen Declaration"* of black churchmen, in the face of the repressive and genocidal racism of American society, might be promulgated by NCNC, with the Theological Commission providing the study basis upon which such an historic declaration might be constructed.

The Commission was directed to go on with the work outlined (mainly in the form of study questions) in its Report. It is the continuation of that work, conducted by correspondence with a group of distinguished black scholars, that is reported in the main body of this document.

Finally, on the eve of the assassination of Dr. Martin Luther King, Jr., the Board of Directors, meeting in Chicago, took action to indicate to the predominantly white churches—especially to their urban mission structure—the implications for mission strategy of the theological reconstruction that was going on in significant sectors of the black Christian community.

That statement on "The Urban Mission in a Time of Crisis" declared that no longer must the white religious establishment bypass black churches in order to make direct contact with the ghetto masses. It called upon white mission structures to "reappraise strategies and expenditures"; to "come to the bargaining table"; and "to surrender resources . . . [for] true partnership with black churchmen . . . in the cities."

*Statement made at Barmen, Germany, by the confessing churches during the Nazi regime.—Ed.

These bold strategy considerations, which have elicited expressions of considerable unhappiness among some white brethren in official circles, were buttressed by four theological or ecclesiological concepts. First the theological, liturgical and missionary renewal of black churches as a "new style" of black church life and mission. Secondly, the development of the black congregation as a "community organization." Thirdly, the projection of the black congregation as a center of black awareness and black culture. And finally, the concept of the messianic role of the black church, authenticated by "its experience of suffering and . . . yearning for freedom."

Thus is it evident in the work of three brief meetings of the NCNC that some important groundwork has been laid for a theological platform of widening scope and increasing depth, albeit unstable and somewhat out of plumb in its present formulation.

The point is not that black churchmen are enunciating in these documents what white churchmen have not or cannot say. That may or may not be, but in either case it is askew of our main concern. What is important is that churchmen who share a common pain and humiliation under the heel of white oppression, who share a common pride and self-awareness, who share a common commitment to militant if not radical resistance to dehumanization and deracination, have lifted up certain ideological and theological fragments, themes and discernments which, when taken together and ordered in a rational conceptual framework, provide a clarification of the motivation for black mobilization and renewal and give us a point of departure for a new dialogue and confrontation with both conservative "whitenized" black Christians and liberal, but paralyzed white Christians, whose accommodations to the religious and secular status quo has all but robbed American Christianity of its vitality and credibility—especially among the poor, the black and the young.

III

During the summer of 1968, informal conversations with several NCNC members who are or who were formerly associated with theological seminaries led to the development, within the Theological Commission, of a list of some 20 black church scholars and theologians—most of whom are presently teaching. One Roman Catholic priest was included in that list.

These persons were invited to participate in a project which would survey their opinions and reactions regarding the theological issues lifted up at the Dallas meeting and those which were reflected in four representative articles written by four persons on the list. Three of the articles have appeared in publications. One is to be published later this year.

The purpose of this project was to make available to NCNC at its St. Louis meeting the considered judgments, of some of the most competent of black church scholarship on a few key questions in the current discussion about a "black theology." It was not assumed that we had either exhausted the most relevant questions, nor that we had communicated with all or even the most knowledgeable black theologians in the nation. It was assumed that if it were possible to get an analysis of some significant theological material from a few established persons in the field, we would be able to surmise with some accuracy how close black scholars were to a consensus on several important matters, what were significant points of disagreement, what lines of development required further study and discussion, what might be the ingredients of a basic NCNC theological position paper, an embryonic confessional statement or a contemporary

pronouncement akin to the Barmen Declaration, the famous Columbus Statement of the Federal Council of Churches in 1936 or *Mater et Magistra* of Pope John XXIII.

In any event, the project has been completed with thirteen persons responding. The main purpose of this report is to share the findings and to comment upon the main themes and ideas which emerge from this collective effort. The continued work of the Theological Commission should, perhaps, be guided by the discussion of this material and additional material at the Second National Convocation. It will be the decision of those NCNC members who work with the Commission in St. Louis whether or not the National Commission should be presented with a draft theological statement this year. Such a statement, if desirable, could be for receipt without approval, adoption as an NCNC policy position or adoption as a study document. There may be, of course, other alternatives.

The following questions were asked of the respondents:

1. Is our traditional assumption of the mystical unity of the church as the Body of Christ incompatible with the creation of NCNC as a separate organization of black churchmen? If not, why not? What is the relationship between the quest for true unity of the Body of Christ and the quest for racial justice?

2. What are the ingredients of a new Christian anthropology which in its definition of true manhood takes seriously the problem of oppressed, subjugated, excluded and emasculated men?

3. How does the doctrine of the suffering servant relate to the necessary acquisition of power by suffering, powerless people? Is there a difference between the post-crucifixion man, the new man

in Jesus Christ and the idea of man seeking to be crucified as an innocent, powerless sacrifice to the world of sin and evil?

4. What Biblical images undergird and substantiate the movement of black churchmen today? The abrahamic pilgrimage, the Exodus, the concept of the Remnant, etc? What new images and redefinition of Biblical images need to be projected by black churchmen?

5. What is the relationship between the orthodox emphasis upon the sacred individuality and uniqueness of a man and his belonging to a group which helps to define his personhood, i.e. his peoplehood, or groupness, or corporateness?

6. Is it theologically valid to speak of a black Christ or a white Christ? Whatever were the historic circumstances under which the Christ figure first appeared, must that historic situation and the elements with which it consists be considered eternally, universally authentic, valid and normative?

7. If God acts in history do we know him within the history of the American experience as slanted by white people or should we seek to understand God in history as black people? What is to be said about the moral integrity of the white interpretation of history?

8. Is there a Christian theory of violence and what would it say about the role of violence in effecting social change?

9. Is there a kind of theory of "soul" which brings together sociological and psychological insights into the nature and quality of the black man's experience of segregation, suffering and victory in the American situation?

10. What is your reaction to the Williams Manuscript?

11. What is your reaction to the Harding article?

12. What is your reaction to the Mitchell article?

13. What is your reaction to the Wilmore manuscript?

On items 1, 3, 2, 9, and 7, there was general agreement, in that order. The strongest agreement, by far, was in the answers to Question 1 (hereafter referred to as Q-1). The writers strongly supported the existence of NCNC as fully compatible with their views on the oneness of the Church.

A typical strong response came from Dr. Grant S. Shockley:

> The traditional assumption of the mystical unity of the church as the Body of Christ is not incompatible with the creation of a National conference of Negro Churchmen or a Black Church Movement. Actually, it may be an essential affirmation of such a teaching. The unity of the Body of Christ is vitiated by the members of that Body who disjoin themselves from others who might be members of it. The mystical unity of the church is that quality of fellowship that ensues when men freely respond to God's call to be gathered into one fellowship of those who would be faithful to him.

But Dr. Shockley's rejoinder does raise at the end of the following quote, a question about the *racial* or *non-racial* meaning of NCNC which appears in almost half of the other responses. How open or how closed are we?

> Actually, unless a Christian fellowship is one in which persons are not denied full equality without distinction it is hardly Christ's Body regardless! This being the case, black churchmen are not only justified but obligated, for the sake of conscience, church and Kingdom to develop whatever structure seems wise and effective to achieve a community of faith that is both loyal to Christ and open to all who desire its fellowship.

Another fairly typical response to Q-1 is that of Dr. Edsel A. Ammons of Evanston, Illinois:

Organization of NCNC as a separate group within the body of Christ is for that reason alone consistent with our witness. Its creation is intended to identify and call into question unjust social systems which deny the sovereignty of Christ, thus rendering impossible the unity which is implicit in our understanding of the meaning of the body of Christ.

True unity obtains only in a climate of accepting love (justing love) in which context the corpus not only distinguishes but also *celebrates* individual uniqueness or differences. Justice, in other words, is the style of the loving, accepting community.

Most respondents saw little of momentous theological relevance in Q-3. Dr. G. Murray Branch replies significantly:

The "post-crucifixion man" or the "new man in Jesus Christ" has the evidence that much good can come through surrender of one's will and one's self to God, but in the absence of an overpowering sense of vocation even post-crucifixion man will not seek crucifixion or even offer himself as a sacrifice for the sins of the world. Moreover, if the servant figure in the Book of Isaiah be understood as representing the elect people, Israel, or the true or best within Israel, then it is even less likely that the suffering servant figure will serve as a pattern, example or inspiration for victimized and powerless Afro-Americans who have no such sense of election, solidarity, mission, or corporate personality.

Rev. Hargett in this connection was more typical in his response:

I see no relationship between the doctrine of the suffering servant and the necessary acquisition of power by suffering, powerless people.

Jesus allowed himself to suffer as a servant to demonstrate how Agape is willing to risk itself in becoming the

significant other. I like the distinction Martin Buber makes in his book entitled "Moses."

He says essentially that we must make a distinction between liberator and martyr.

Q-2 received general agreement along the lines indicated in the following quote from Dr. Henry H. Mitchell, of Santa Monica:

A new Christian anthropology must needs emphasize the text "NOW are we [ALL] the sons of God, even if yet it does not appear what we shall be."

To the black man himself, there must be more emphasis on the sense of divine destiny, a suffering servant who suffers for his militance in seeking to save his brother of the lighter skin from racism. The sense of vocation can be stated in the modern context in terms of Toynbee's internal proletariat. Without equal power, they seem to determine the course of whole civilizations anyway. This must be seen as God's way of honoring and using men, and as an antidote for the subtle and unvoiced anti-Christian anthropology of the Black Man who does not even believe our report when we say God loves and accepts him

Q-7 and Q-9 dealt with God in black history and a possible theology of soul, rexpectively. There was general agreement that we must discover God in our own history and almost all respondents could see only vague outlines of a "theology of soul."

Dr. Ammons, however, makes a rather untypical comment on Q-7:

Two things need to be said and kept in mind in the interest of the integrity of black people as they endeavor to appropriate the facts of history. *First, all white distortions or misinterpretation of history are not intentional.* White persons are products of a history, particularly in the American culture, which has long legitimized historical distortions and which bequeathes to its young such distortions. Most whites, therefore, deal with questions of social and cultural history in ways which have been predetermined by factors within their own environmental situations. Morality or lack of moral integrity in relation to their handling of historical data must be weighed in relation to those facts.

A second thing to remember is that the question which is really before us has to do with the problem of human sense. Every man, white or black, is the creature of his culture and unless made especially sensitive *will by the very nature of things be unable to know of the extent of his participation and any historical distortions.*

Rev. Lawrence E. Lucas, the Roman Catholic brother whose replies were among the most "radical," is forceful on Q-7:

I think it's extremely difficult to know Christ within the history of the American experience as created by the white man. We have no choice but to seek to understand God in our history as black people. Only after this, can we see Him in the broader context.

What can be said about the moral integrity of the white interpretation of history is simply to point out that there is precious little of moral integrity in this interpretation.

While there was a general affirmation on Q-9, there were many "perhaps" and some indication of not understanding. Several pushed for universalization Dr. C. Shelby Rooks:

Of course, "soul" has sociological, psychological, and humanistic connotations and elements. The black man's experiences in the world, and particularly in America, do have elements that transcend the normal separation of men. The commonality of the black experiences forge a bond not unlike that known by the Jews in Israel. What is as yet unknown is the ultimate result of the oneness that black people feel. It is probable that slaves in other lands and times felt something of the same kinship. But not all of the slave experiences resulted in a positive contribution to human history. Slaves in other parts of the world revolted and were sometimes wiped out. In other cases, they were freed and were assimilated into the population. In still other instances, they finally created their own nations and societies.

What needs exploration is the quality and bases of the kinship that oppressed people feel and an examination of the effect these have upon the eventual life of the oppressed community. There may well be a direct correlation between the quality of "soul" and an eventually successful community and life.

The most interesting points of *disagreement* were in Q-4, 5, 6, and 8. On Q-4, many did approve the images cited in the question but several brought in diverse images for consideration. Dr. Charles B. Copher, whose paper was in some ways the most cautious, made this comment:

First of all, I should say that, according to my view and interpretation of the Bible, there are no Biblical images which undergird and substantiate the movement of black (or any other) churchmen. Today, perhaps such images may be legitimately appropriated for many reasons. Along this latter procedure, many images are suitable. Among them are the following: The Abrahamic Pilgrimage and Faith; Moses in his Call and Leadership; The Challenge of Joshua—choose you this day; The Covenant People; The Remnant People, etc., from the Old Testament; A New Man in Christ, and Heirs of the Promise (Hebrews), from the New Testament.

At this time, I cannot think of new images that need to be projected. To be sure, all the Biblical images would have to be redefined and applied. This latter would have to be done, however, in the light of the universal nature of the Christian faith.

Again, Lucas' response is at variance:

All of these images play a part. Other images and concepts needing emphasis are: an emphasis on the living black Christ now calling and gathering His people, black people, for the reformation of themselves, and through them the country and the world; not only the peace that Christ has come to bring but also the violence involved in the creating of a true and meaningful peace; the new man image and the need for self-consciousness and identity; the concept of the new community; the purpose and destiny of that new community; the concept of messiah and the need for black messiah; the concept of God's judgment and the role of the community of God regarding that judgment; recreating and constantly renovating and changing that world; the concept of resurrection and resurrection as a source of power and glory. These are but some suggestions.

Almost half of the writers seem to conceive, as Dr. Branch put it, "of no ultimate uniqueness inherent in man." In other words, they chose to put stress upon "groupness" or "peoplehood" as the significant and defining context of personal existence.

Rooks, for one of the other group, however, sees dangers in this emphasis so much in vogue these days among black nationalists who speak of "folk spirit" and "accountability to the black community."

There is a kind of urgency to this question. More and more black Christians in America are called upon to conform to developing group norms. More and more they are required to give their assent to the methodology of the more radical revolutionists among black people. There is a drift toward community separation, toward violence, toward the denial of our common brotherhood with white men that the Gospel (as distinct from Christian practice and tradition) proclaims. Some segments of the black community are demanding that every black individual must sacrifice everything of himself for the development of the community. All of these ideas force the issue of ultimate accountability for the individual.

It has been traditional in Christian history that the final arbiter of this question shall be individual conscience. If that is maintained, it is highly likely that there may soon be black martyrs at the hands of black people. But the problem of balance between this Scylla and Charybdis will remain to plague the movement for a long time to come. It is an unresolved question of human experience.

An interesting division ensued over Q-6 dealing with the black Christ. Here the pastors seem to lean toward affirmation with most of the teachers regarding the idea negatively. For example, writes Ammons:

In my judgment we can make no valid claim for a black Christ or a white Christ. Just like the Jews could not lay claim solely to Christ. In fact, the biblical understanding of the Christ is as a Universal figure the incarnate love of God active and involved in the affairs of man.

Also Dr. Frank T. Wilson, former Dean of Howard Divinity School, writes:

Imputation of blackness or whiteness to Christ seems to have no point. Where this has been invoked in support of racism it is sheer blasphemy.
We cannot alter the historic situation under which the Christ figure appeared, nor can we twist the figure to suit a need for "status by association" or to establish the authenticity of the black man's integral "being" in the Body of Christ.

On the other hand, note the responses of pastors Mitchell and Lucas, respectively, from two of the most diverse theological traditions in the group:

While the historic elements of the Christ figure include pigmentation and the probability of hair like unto Lamb's wool, this does not make such normative. The fact that Christ was so real to Sallman that he made Jesus a man of his own culture and race is a fact that must be paralleled in all races and cultures, if we seriously mean that he is to reign over all and that his lordship is universal.

I think it is, if theology is to relate realistically with life. In our present context, we are involved more with the resurrected, living Christ, rather than the historical Christ. The historic circumstances under which the Christ figure first appeared must be considered eternally, universally authentic, valid, normative, revelatory, etc. However, it is under the present circumstance that this Christ is now being Himself. In so far as white "Christians" have distorted this Christ into a white Christ interested only in subjugating, exploiting black people, I think it is valid to speak in terms of present realities of a black Christ to correct this distortion.

Again, disagreements appear on the issue of violence, dividing the respondents almost down the middle. The negative representatives below are Copher and Rooks, respectively.

The extent to which a theory is Christian is open to question, and there is no agreement among Christians with respect to the right answer or answers. I, myself, cannot condone violence as a means of effecting social change—except as employed legally by a representative, duly constituted government.

To talk about a "Christian" theory of violence is to distort the picture of Christ that has come down to us in the Biblical account and in tradition. About the only place in the Bible where Jesus used physical violence was in chasing the money-changers out of the Temple. Everywhere else, he is a man of compassion using his words and his deeds to transform men's thinking. He is a healer of the sick, a sufferer with men in their conditions, a man profoundly concerned about what to him was essential: man's relationship to God.

On the other side, see the following quotations from the papers of Father Lucas, Dr. L. L. Haynes of Baton Rouge and Dr. John H. Satterwhite, respectively:

The Roman Catholic tradition to which I belong has set this down in a set of principles around the notion of the "just war" and "legitimate self-defense." Violence out of passion or its morality is judged more in terms of the circumstances leading to the passionate outburst and its causes and responsibilities. I suggest that in these circumstances, the greater responsibility lies on those who are more responsible for the conditions under which black people are revolting.

On the principles of legitimate self defense, I think the deliberate, planned type of violence can be morally justified and violence can be or play a role in effecting social change. The social change is not seen as moving from the good to the better but in putting an end to systemic violence and therefore self defense.

Violence does play a role in social change. The Christian sometimes submits himself to violence knowing that every human action is involved with the contradictions of sin. Faith in the goodness of God is not to be equated with confidence in the virtue of man. The Christian therefore sees a good God working his will even in and through violence. A crucified Christ is a momentary defeat but not an ultimate victory. When systems tend to destroy rather than help life, they must be destroyed.

There are situations where Christians may become involved in violence as an ultimate recourse which is justified only in extreme situations. The use of violence requires a rigorous definition of the ends to which it is used, and a clear recognition of the evils which are inherent in it and it should be tempered by mercy.

For the most part, all of the responses to the questions in this section of the survey instrument were fairly balanced. Answers tended to avoid feeling-responses and were based upon assumed rational and systematic treatments without being pedantic. Generally speaking, the writiers were more in harmony with one another than in disagreement with wide areas of tentative or open-ended judgments. The one clear consensus was emphasis upon the *distinctive* needs of black Christians for unity, self-awareness and social justice.

The writers also gave reactions to four articles written by Preston Williams, Vincent Harding, Henry Mitchell and Gayraud Wilmore. Space does not permit a précis of each article to be included in this document. They dealt with various aspects of black religion and issues associated with the history, future and mission strategy of black churches.

One or two key concerns in the most controversial articles may be briefly considered here. For example, Mitchell's article, "Black Power and the Christian Church" (*Baptist Journal of History and Theology*, 1968), received this comment from Dr. Lawrence Jones, Dean of Union Theological Seminary—fairly representative of other reactions to Mitchell:

Mr. Mitchell's attempt to deal with the "positive portrayal" of black religion is an admirable one. He speaks with great certainty about the "corpus of black religious tradition in America." I would like to know where the body is hidden (if indeed he is referring to a deposit of literature). Black churchmen have been singularly remiss in developing a "corpus" that is accessible to those who study in this area. I do not doubt that much material exists but it is in remote and unknown places, in church headquarters, dusty attics, and moldy basements. To one who has tried to teach a course informed in part by some of Mitchell's assumptions, this lack of material is a "stone of stumbling." It is commonplace where black clergy gather to hear long dissertations on the genius of black worship, but the documentation for the dissertations is more often than not part poetry, part testimony, part exaggeration, part embroidered

memory, and part personal history. As fascinating as all of this is, it is hardly the substance for the study of black religion. One can speak from his own experience but one dares not generalize too broadly from this limited base.

Some of the most critical analysis of the articles came from Dr. Joseph R. Washington, of Albion College, the distinguished author of *Black Religion* (which Preston Williams' article takes to task for his concept of the origin and nature of black religion) and *The Politics of God* (Boston: Beacon Press, 1967).

Dr. Washington, as well as others, acknowledged the superiority of the Harding manuscript on "The Religion of Black Power" (in *The Religions Situation, 1968*) while expressing some perplexity (as did others) of where Dr. Harding actually comes out on the future of the black church and his own personal commitment to it as an agency of revolution in the American situation. Washington makes the following comment on the Harding article:

Is Black Power a religion seeking a theology? If so, Black Power as religion and the traditional religion of black churchmen are diametrically opposed. This writer has suggested some theological dimensions of Black Power which cannot be set forth here without taking a hold of the full meaning of Black Power, not just what some would like it to be—forthcoming in a book to be published. For now, however, Professor Harding's article is important if black theologians are serious about developing black theology on the coattails of Black Power. Their difficulty may be increased by the awareness that Mr. Harding embraces fully neither Black Power nor religion but wishes to divest them both of essentials in line with his philosophical position that carefully weaves between Black Power and the authentic religion of black people. In choosing what is meaningful for him in Black

Power and in religion both are reduced to grist for his mill. What is certain is that he makes clear that Black Power and the institutional concerns of black churchmen are only incidentally related. A theology for black people as God's chosen people is possible and necessary. A theology of Black Power is, apart from black people, about as significant as a theology of democracy or communism—they may be viewed as a religion but they have more credence as political and economic theories. The connection between Black Power and the religion of black people or black religion is the experience of black people and not the ecclesiastical expressions.

On the controversial question surrounding the publication of his first book, tender spots opened up by both the Williams and the Mitchell articles. Dr. Washington has this interesting and informative comment to make with obvious significance for the development of NCNC:

> Black Religion is rightly criticized in its lack of sympathy for black churches qua black churches, but it is not to be missed that equal condemnation is made of white churches qua white churches. Black Religion was not wrong in calling a spade a spade, it did not however win favor by calling it a damn black spade. This was neither wise nor judicious, but the book was not written to win admirers, it was written to provoke black churchmen into awareness and response in change for the best. The position Washington holds is that the greatness is not black churches or black theology—they are not defended therefore. Washington's position in Black Religion and in The Politics of God is that greatness is in black people qua black people. Their institutional expressions may not measure up to their greatness, but radical changes will come about through the people who are black, irrespective of their allegiances vis-à-vis ideologies, theologies, and philosophies. Defensiveness of black ecclesiastical institutions is a misplaced emphasis. The day may not be past when their institutional expressions of historic standing are on

the forefront, but, it is certain that attunement must be made to the black people and not institutions. Those who place priority on black institutions over black people or who hold that the two are inseparable are defending the wrong substance of black power. Black power is black people. Institutions may be instrumental thereto. They are indispensible, but they are not sacred. The Protestant principle is that nothing is sacred, beyond criticism. We need a radical theology for a radical black people and this does not come about through self-congratulatory togetherness.

The controversial issue in Wilmore's article ("The Case for a New Black Church Style") was evidently the elaboration of the idea which appeared in the Urban Crisis statement of the NCC Board of Directors, namely that the black Church must also become a "community organization," in the IFCO* sense. Several writers raised questions about this assumption. Dr. Edsel A. Ammons writes:

> I would argue only with the author's conclusion that the black church must develop "as a community organization." My own experiences suggest the impossibility, if not the undesirability, of this goal. In the first place, too many non-church people are frightened away by the evidence of church domination of such structure. And the caliber of leadership (preferably lay leadership) demanded by the magnitude of the task is all too often conspicuous by its absence from our churches. Churches, it would seem, ought to undertake to identify the needs and commit their resources to the support of an existing organization serving the community (free of partisan church ties) where they do exist or of a representative group from the community which may be encouraged to initiate an organizing

*Interreligious Foundation for Community Organization, Inc.—Ed.

effort. The kinds of moralistic trivia in which congregational groups engage wherever issues are controversial in nature would all too often nullify the work of a community organization as it engages in the complex and often ambiguous politics of city and municipal government.

The most generally appreciated article was the contribution of Dr. Preston Williams of Boston Theological Seminary, who wrote on "Black Church: Origin, History, Present Dilemmas." Dr. Shelby Rooks makes a pointed reaction to his major thesis:

Dr. Williams makes the pertinent point that this development of Christianity traces its origins neither solely to African religion brought to these shores by slaves nor to American Protestantism as it was portrayed to the slaves by whites. To each of these strains black Christians in America owe something; but a more careful analysis may show that we are dealing with a religious phenomenon which is not just a synthesis of the two strains mentioned above, but the creation of something entirely different that bears some similarities to other religious experiences in America.

Up to this point, most church historians have been content either to ignore the black religious phenomena in this country or simply to relate it to the early frontier religion.

Williams is quite right in suggesting that neither of these responses is the accurate one. Instead, a whole new approach to the study of black Christian history may suggest an entirely different thesis: that the experience of slavery and segregation has enabled the black American to sustain the essential Biblical understanding of the Judaeo-Christian faith while the rest of American Protestantism has been busy distorting it.

Dr. Grant Shockley wrote at length and more critically on this paper:

Williams makes a strong case for the need of the black man in America to acknowledge and develop his African religious heritage. While he recognizes the difficulty in recovering and appropriating such a past, he feels strongly that this must be done. One can quite agree with this basic need to build on what is inherent and indigenous. It must be stressed, however, that a knowledge of this past is all but irrevocable. Probably the most that it has bequeathed us is an ethos, the content and details of which must be recalled and redeveloped in and by the black experience in America.

Black Religion as Protest—

By far the strongest part of the Williams paper is this section on protest. He points out in this connection that this protest never became more than "protest," i.e., initiative for reform. Except in the case of individuals, e.g., Henry Garnett, the Negro Church has always been dangerously close to the category of basically conservative institutions seeking to "reform" the white church and white society. It seems to me that this questions the model of the Negro Church in any of its historical periods to fashion or guide the Revolution to which Williams claims it should be giving its attention today.

The Future of Black Religion—

Williams is probably correct in his pessimism about the future of black religion based on the *present* Negro Church. He correctly calls for a new black theology that is not color "racist" but "soul" black "racial." Admirable is the use of the newer trend in theology toward the secularization of the church which Williams employs to gain new and needed leverage for a relevant black church for, of and by black people and any who can and will so identify themselves with it.

IV

What conclusions can be drawn from these reactions, taken as a whole? Are unities or patterns here which may suggest currents of black scholarship and therefore offer guidance to the theological development of the NCNC and the black caucuses of several denominations?

The writer is not sure. One thing, however, seems clear. It is the lively interest and enthusiasm black academicians and pastors have for breaking into what has obviously been a quiescent, almost sterile theological orthodoxy among black churches of all denominations. There is, unquestionably, great interest in opening up new material for theological study and reconstruction among black churchmen.

There is a sneaking suspicion among those who participated in the project that something is stirring in parts of the black church; that there is a kind of "black theology" aborning, equal to the budding renaissance in arts and letters which is heralded today in Harlem and other black communities across the nation. All of the respondents in this survey welcomed this new quest for the theological basis of black church renewal in the context of the movement for racial justice. They see it as appropriate, authentic, and requiring no special justification before God or church councils.

The basic issues that all of these men are wrestling with can be stated in the following questions: What is the distinctive, unique and authoritative meaning of "blackness" in the context of historic Christianity? Put another way: Does the black church have "anything going for it" (as does black music, humor, fiction, business, education, etc.) today that sets it apart as an indispensably viable institution, not only of the black community, but of American society generally? Can it be the primary instrument for the liberation of black people in this country and perhaps in Asia, Africa, and Latin America as well, and, if so, to what extent will this necessitate a break with the fundamental norms, styles and structures of mainline, white American Christianity?

These are serious questions which plague the black Christian scholar today and that they are uppermost in the minds of those who took part in the NCNC Theological Project is amply demonstrated in the substance and tone of the reactions given to the material submitted by the Theological Commission. They cannot be answered superficially and it may take years of concentrated theological study and discussion to properly shape the right questions, much less the answers. Thus the timely relevance of the urgent concern about recruiting black youth to church vocations—particularly to seminary teaching and research.

In the judgment of the writer three tentative conclusions can be drawn from this survey:

(1) As stated above, there is great interest in, but some uncertainty about the unique and distinctive qualities of black religion and churchmanship which distinguish it from the acculturated white types which are part of the American system of oppression and racism. There is, nevertheless, some glimmerings here of an incipient black interpretation of Christology, the nature and the mission of the Church in a world dominated by White Power.

(2) Even if, as with most of the writers in this project, there is talk of the "gospel of Blackness" (Harding) or "soul theology" no radical changes from what may be thought of as main line Reformation theology and ethics are suggested by the formulations contained in these papers. Vincent Harding's article may be the one notable exception by virtue of his discussion of self-love and universalism based on suffering, struggle and hope rather than on "common links to a possible dead Creator-Father." But on the whole, even

in the discussion of glorification, resurrection, self-defense, Messianism, etc., Harding himself does not break radical new ground that may, for example, earn the designation of a new black heresy vis-à-vis traditional Christianity.

None of the respondents go as far, for example, as Dr. Albert Cleage, in a radical redefinition of the Christian faith. With few exceptions they reach back for a purer version of "the faith once delivered to the Apostles," but corrupted by the culture religion of both blacks and whites.

(3) For the most part, these scholars see the peculiarities and integrities of "the black experience" as matters of sociological rather than theophanic or even theonomous significance. This does not mean that they are not held to be important. It simply means that the secularization of the church is positively construed and regarded to be so far advanced by these writers that they see no good reason to value some residual spirituality or devotionalism in the black community.

The trends that Dr. Ruby F. Johnson recognized as early as 1956 in her *The Religion of Negro Protestants*—a diminution of nonempirical elements and the coordination of religion with various aspects of the practical life—seem well advanced and confirmed in the theological outlook of the respondents to this survey. By far the most noteworthy characteristic of these papers is the emphasis upon the church as a social institution dedicated to the pursuit of freedom, justice and material well-being for oppressed peoples. Its special relationship today to the Black Power movement —i.e., the black man's quest for solidarity, pride and political and economic power— is broadly recognized by this group. How that relationship should be legitimated theologically and how it should be strengthened and made more strategic for the liberation struggle and the renewal of the church remains for all of us to ponder and hopefully agree upon in the days ahead.

APPENDIX E

THE BLACK PAPER

from *THE FINDINGS OF BLACK METHODIST FOR CHURCH RENEWAL, 1968*

I. Our Confession

We, a group of black Methodists in America, are deeply disturbed about the crisis of racism in America. We are equally concerned about the failure of a number of black people, including black Methodists to respond appropriately to the roots and forces of racism and the current Black Revolution.

We, as black Methodists, must first respond in a state of confession because

it is only as we confront ourselves that we are able to deal with the evils and forces which seek to deny our humanity.

We confess our failure to be reconciled with ourselves as black men. We have too often denied our blackness (hair texture, color and other God-given physical characteristics) rather than embrace it in all its black beauty.

We confess that we have not always been relevant in service and ministry to our black brothers, and in so doing we have alienated ourselves from many of them.

We confess that we have not always been honest with ourselves and with our white brothers. We have not encountered them with truth but often with deception. We have not said in bold language and forceful action that, "You have used 'white power' in and outside of the church to keep us in a subordinate position." We have failed to tell our white brothers "like it is!" Instead, we have told our white brothers what we thought they would like to hear.

We confess that we have not become significantly involved in the Black Revolution because, for the most part, white men have defined it as "bad," for the other part, we have been too comfortable in our "little world," too pleased with our lot as second-class citizens and second-class members of The Methodist Church.

We confess that we have accepted too long the philosophy of racism. This has created a relationship in which white people have always defined the "terms," and, in fact, defined when and how black people would exist.

We confess that we have accepted a "false kind of integration" in which all power remained in the hands of white men.

II. The Black Revolution

"The Black Revolution is a fact! It is a call for black people throughout the nation and the world to stand on their feet and declare their independence from white domination and exploitation. The mood of the day is for black people to throw off the crippling myths of white superiority and black inferiority. The old myths are being replaced by black pride

self-development, self-awareness, self-respect, self-determination and black solidarity."*

We are new men—the old man,—"nigger," is dead. The "boy" is now a man!

We now stand as proud black men prepared to embrace our blackness and committed to address ourselves unequivocally and forcefully to racism wherever we find it, in and outside the church.

III. Black Power

How then do we respond forcefully and responsibly to racism in America and racism in The United Methodist Church?

"It is abundantly clear to many Americans that power is basic to all human dynamics. The fundamental distortion facing us in a controversy about 'black power' is rooted in a gross imbalance of power and conscience between Negroes and white Americans. It is this distortion, mainly, which is responsible for the widespread, though, often inarticulate, assumption that white people are justified in getting what they want through the use of power, but that Negro Americans must, either by nature or by circumstance, make their appeal only through conscience. As a result, the power of white men and the conscience of black men have both been corrupted."†

Black power provides the means by which black people do for themselves that which no other group can do for them.

". . . Black power speaks to the need for black people to move from the stands of

*Archie Rich, "The Black Methodist's Response to Black Power," (a mimeographed paper prepared for the National Conference of Negro Methodists, Cincinnati, Ohio, February 6–9, 1968).

†"Statement of Black Power," (a mimeographed paper developed by the National Committee of Negro Churchmen, July 31, 1966).

humble, dependent and impotent beggars to the stature of men who will take again into their own hands, as all men must, the fashioning of their own destiny for their own growth into self-development and self-respect."*

Black power is a call for black people in this country to unite, to recognize their heritage, and to build a sense of community. It is a call for us to take the initiative, to build the kind of community which crosses all class lines and geographical lines, in order that the resources and leadership of all black people may be used.

Black power means the development and utilization of the gifts of black men for the good of black men and the whole nation.

Finally, it is a call for us to respond to God's action in history which is to make and keep human life human.

IV. Black Power
and the
United Methodist Church

We, as black Methodists, affirm the search for black identity. When we affirm and embrace our blackness we are acknowledging what God has done and we no longer wear our blackness as a stigma, but as a blessing.

"In religious terms, a God of power, of majesty and of might, who has made man to be in His own image and likeness, must will that His creation reflect in the immediacies of life His power, His majesty and His might. Black power raises, for the healing of humanity and for the renewal of commitment to the creative religious purpose of growth, the far too long overlooked need for power, if life is to

become what in the mind of its Creator it is destined to be."*

Therefore, as black Methodists, if we are obedient to God's creation, we have a responsibility to ourselves, the white community and to white Methodists to relate from a position of power.

The Methodist church has failed institutionally and spiritually to be the church. It has refused to take seriously its mission to redeem all mankind. It has denied the black man's right to self-determination because it has frustrated his quest for self-realization. It has failed in every respect to see the black man as a child of God. The reality has been that the black man is denied full membership in the institutional church.

We as black Methodists, reaffirm our belief in God and His church. We believe that all men are brothers and that God is our Father. However, we see the possibility that "white" Christians in general, and white Methodists in particular, may not be seriously committed to the church or the concept of the brotherhood of man under the fatherhood of God. We therefore have a responsibility under God to bring about renewal in the church at all levels of its existence. The thrust of "black power" in this context is to awaken black and white Methodists so they might come to see and carry out the mission of the church as it relates to all men. The United Methodist Church ought to be sensitive to every segment of society. It should minister realistically and effectively to the total needs of men —especially those who have been dispossessed by society and the church. Black power seeks to be the moving force behind the black man's effort to get the church to see and recognize him. A second aim of black power in The United

*Nathan Wright, Jr., *Black Power and Urban Unrest* (New York: Hawthorne Books, Inc., 1967), p. 60.

*Nathan Wright, Jr., *Black Power and Urban Unrest* (New York: Hawthorne Books, Inc., 1967), p. 136.

Methodist Church is to help the dispossessed, especially the black man, to establish his selfhood in society and in the church.

To do this we propose that black and white Methodists across the country mobilize their spiritual, intellectual, economic, social and political resources in order to exert the necessary influence and/or pressure upon the power structures of The United Methodist Church on all levels to bring about change and renewal in order that it might unconditionally include all Methodists in its total Life. At the same time we propose to preach the Gospel of the "somebodiness" of the black man so that those who have not "identified" themselves as men might find that identity and exert their manhood.

We hope that this can be done within the new framework of the United Methodist Church. As for black Methodists, we are determined to serve God by redeeming our brothers, which in turn redeems us.

THE ROLE OF THE LOCAL CHURCH

The local church in the black community must immediately redefine its own structure and life in terms of its ability to minister to the black community. If necessary, the local church should not hesitate to restructure itself in order to minister to its community, whether or not the restructuring reflects existing Methodist policy. In order that the totality of man's existence (for which the local church is concerned) may be seen as the arena for local church involvement, any redefinition plans should include an examination of all current movements and organizations such as those related to civil rights, social and economic justice, peace and general welfare.

I. Principles Regarding Local Church Staff Financing

A. It is necessary to have more direct "benevolent" giving from the black church to salaries of church staffs in order to compete effectively with agencies in and outside of the church for the best black leadership available.

B. Churches in a given area (parish, district, conference) should develop salary equalization plans, thus making it possible for church staffs to be assigned and utilized where need is apparent without undergoing financial jeopardy.

II. Local Church and Black Culture

The local church should undertake a program of creative teaching about the black man's contributions to the building of America, and nations throughout the world. This effort would include the collection of books and periodicals, contemporary and otherwise, written about African and Afro-American accomplishments; thus, making the local church a resource and surveyor of black culture.

III. The Local Church Community

The local church must look upon its task in the black community to be so crucial that the church initiates plans to establish team ministries in every congregation in the community. Such teams composed of clergy and laity, should be organized on the task force basis, providing special functions as legal services, employment counseling, cooperative buying, extra-educational programs, and community organization.

IV. Effective Educational Programming

A. The following educational styles should be introduced to local congregations:

1. establish courses of study on the black church to be used in schools of mission and other educational settings (e.g., E. Franklin Frazier, The Negro Church in America,

Joseph R. Washington, Black Religion: The Negro and Christianity in the United States).

2. educate churchmen relative to the role of the church in the midst of violence.

3. educate for the redefinition of ministry in the black community to include concern for the totality of man's existence and the community's needs.

4. establish programs of political action using pertinent community issues, such as inadequate schools, sanitation problems, election, etc.

B. Educational innovations for local church staffs should include:

1. establishing training programs for effective staff efforts in the black community.

2. establishing courses in urban and rural sociology, each in its appropriate setting; and courses in administration for mission.

3. establishing programs linking pastors and laymen of different churches ("partners in learning") to utilize a variety of experiences and resources.

4. supporting mandatory "refresher-educational" opportunities for all local church staff, no less than one opportunity each quadrennium.

V. The Local Church— Creative Power

A. Programs and policies of all general boards and agencies of The United Methodist Church must be designed and/or implemented to insure the placement of black men at all levels of involvement in those agencies. Local churches can indicate this concern to the Methodist Publishing House and its affiliates, for example, through their support and purchases of church school materials, hymnals, clerical vestments, etc.

B. Utilizing this purchasing power, local churches must also insist that Methodist literature present a more composite account of black people, especially of their participation in The United Methodist Church.

VI. The Local Church and Economic Independence—"Action Toward the Transformation of the System"— Recommendations for Black Methodists

A. Pooling of financial resources for specific tasks which take priority in the black community. Such action might involve the following methods:

1. channeling a percentage of, or all of, the benevolence apportionment of a local church to local communal projects undertaken in alliance with other black congregations in a local community.

2. establishing a national fund (a portion of the above to be channeled to a national fund) in order to assist in those communities where personal involvement in situations has been threatened; and in order to aid communal projects in any of the nation deemed in need of national support.

B. Establish the means of initiating and responding to measures employed by "the system." Insure communal responsibility by seeing that:

1. each local church assess its own situation and undertake such actions as suggested in VI, A, only after having communicated a declaration of intention to appropriate representatives of "the system," and to the continuing body, Black Methodists for Church Renewal.

2. each church agrees upon a means of accountability. When action sugges-

ted in VI, A and B, is undertaken, each church should consent to answer for those actions in the name of the black community.

3. responses to measures employed by the system be developed out of the black community's self-interest and strengths. It is in the black community's self-interest to survive in and for its chosen purposes; to realize its own peace and order; to protect itself.

Therefore, let all responses of the system be assessed by the black brothers in the community. Let him whose individual actions jeopardize the community, and whose actions were without the consensus of the brothers, be liable to the judgement of the brothers.

WHAT ANNUAL CONFERENCES AND DISTRICTS MUST DO TO FREE BLACK METHODIST CHURCHES FOR MINISTRY TO BLACK COMMUNITIES

I. Annual conferences and districts of The United Methodist Church must become informed about the following facts:

A. that black communities are ours to claim as black Methodists; if we cannot and do not claim them, no other community or people can.

B. That presently black Methodist churches are not free to minister to the black communities because:

1. the institutional church drains too much of the financial and professional resources from black churches to insure viable alternatives for creative service to black communities.
2. the available staff persons in local black churches are too involved in institutional "housekeeping" to lend themselves to developing creative programs of service for black people who need them.

C. That financial resources of Methodism are not properly channeled to aid local black churches in ministering to black communities. The following accepted practices verify this finding:

1. present rules regarding church extension monies limit this fund's use to new suburban communities and not to newly-occupied communities resulting from change.
2. present experimental ministries are largely detached from local black churches and are controlled in most instances, by white leadership.

II. Annual conferences and districts must make the following changes to relevantly serve the black communities:

A. Re-define principles of church extension regarding new churches, so as to include financial support of changes in changing communities.

B. Change the strategy of the Urban Departments so that funds for experimental ministries can be made available and channeled through bona fide black churches in order to strengthen their outreach and ministry to the black communities surrounding them.

C. Urban Departments should discontinue and discourage the present policy of support to floating detached, white-controlled organizations providing resources designated for black communities, while such resources are not related to bona fide black churches. Black leadership is top priority for urban ministries.

D. Black churchmen in all black communities should develop programs of ministry to the black communities and suggest means by which resources may be secured from local and connectional funding agencies.

E. A more equitable procedure should be developed to adequately apportion benevolences to churches.

*III. The following are positive actions
from black churchmen which should
be anticipated by
annual conferences and districts:*

A. Black participation on all conference
and district commissions, committees or
agencies.

B. Black ongoing organization to insure
that needs of black people are met.

C. A demand for the voices of black
people to be heard.

*IV. Funds from annual conference
sources should be secured to develop
new and improved ministries for the
black church. This means:*

A. Strengthen present parish ministries:

1. by employing business manager for
   cluster churches which would make
   for better stewardship. Through better record-keeping, buying collec-
   tively, and utilizing fund-raising
   resources, excessive overhead pay-
   ments could be rechanneled to
   program emphasis.

2. by developing a counseling ministry
   which would make available professional help for families and for other
   situations needing such services.

3. by employing qualified and sensitive
   persons who would minister to
   youth, especially in crisis periods.

4. by planning in-service training to
   prepare laymen for work in poverty
   areas, and for tasks not reserved for
   the ordained clergy.

5. by developing cooperative, ecumenical ministries to obtain maximum
   use of existing church facilities, and
   maximum coverage of parish area,
   thus enabling a significantly strengthened leadership to emerge.

B. Outreach beyond local parish:

1. development of store-front ministry
   which would:
   a. encourage involvement and out-
      reach on the part of the local
      congregation.
   b. enable people in the store-front
      area to participate in determin-
      ing their own destiny.
   c. serve as a liaison between the
      middle-class Negro and the poor
      Negro.

2. development of a housing task force
   to secure funds to build federally-
   financed housing for senior citizens
   and low-income persons.

3. establishment of child care for working parents, and Headstart Centers.

4. development of direct action ministry to employ staff person to serve
   as liaison between churches and community organizations, city hall,
   and/or penal institutions. His
   function will be that of channeling
   information to local churches,
   suggesting involvement and action.

5. development of special ministries to
   serve the particular needs such as
   ministries to alcoholics, prostitutes,
   addicts, broken families, divorces,
   delinquents, potential suicides, and
   rural immigrants to the city.

C. Strategy for implementing the
concerns mentioned above:

1. careful study of local church to
   determine its specific needs for a
   stronger parish ministry, and for
   a stronger ministry to the poor.

2. petition proper conference agency
   for funds. Go through all the proper
   channels.

3. withhold payment of benevolence
   funds to achieve these goals when
   all other approaches to secure
   assistance fail.

BLACK RELIGION
PAST, PRESENT AND FUTURE

Position Paper Submitted by the
Philadelphia Council of Black Clergy, 1968

Introductory Statement

Each of the world's cultures has at least one religious expression, barring a few exceptions. Consequently, it is natural that in the development of the American culture, several religious expressions won the acceptance of many Americans. However, it is the Christian religion that was and is the dominant religious expression of the American people.

When one describes the Christian religious expression of the United States of America, he has to take into account its several different religious slants. These are as varied as there are blends of the American way of life. According to Robert Williams' study of the *American Society,** religious freedom prevailed in early America even though nobody intended it.

The task with which this paper is concerned is to establish a position for the Christian expression as it relates to American Black people.

One is not overstating the case by indicating the Christian religious expression has won the acceptance of the great majority of Black people. It is also true that the Christian religion, as it is practiced among white and Black people, is currently under great criticism. Much of this criticism is justified. Some of it is due to an inadequate analysis of the American social system and the significant role the Christian religion has played among Black people in their struggle to

survive. Because of several legitimate frustrations with many of the alleged humanizing institutions in American society, the Christian religion being one, that failed to function in a manner to challenge the racial oppression of Black people, many are now wanting "to throw the baby out with the bath water." This is unfortunate but understandable.

The honest fact about the American Christian religion is that it is a "creation" of white society. This religion has been promulgated to the advantage of white society both in the good it has secured for whites as well as the inhuman acts it has rendered against Black people since 1619. However, the reality of the Christian religion has been contrary to the teachings of its source, Jesus Christ. His life symbolizes what the Christian expression is supposed to be. His ministry was almost a complete contrast to the practice of the Christian religion in the Western world following the second century. He served the poor, alienated, dejected, rejected, and the oppressed people of His society. Jesus was a beautiful human being. The gospels, which record His acts among men, clearly show Jesus to be against any force that denied to any man the full expression of life. In fact, the gospels show Jesus confronting the establishment in the interest of the rejected and the oppressed.

It is true that Black Christian leaders were taught the Christian religious

*Williams, Robert M., Jr. *American Society: A Sociological Interpretation*, Alfred A. Knopf, Inc., 1960, pp 340-344.

103

expression by the white man. This version was biased in support of white society. It should also be noted that many Black ministers of the Christian religion and its followers were even denied the privilege of reading the Bible. As a result, it was difficult for Black men to learn first-hand about Jesus and His ministry; however, there were both freedmen and freemen who became learned leaders. Many of these persons were Christian ministers, among whom were Peter Williams, Jr., and Nathaniel Paul.* Nathaniel Paul understood the Christian religion and used it to strike hard against slavery. He stated in a speech delivered in 1827: "It [slavery] is so contrary to the laws which the God of nature has laid down as the rule of action by which the conduct of man is to be regulated towards his fellow man, which binds him to love his neighbor as himself, that it ever has, and ever will meet the decided disapprobation of heaven."†

Another example of this kind of courageous witness was when the Reverend Absalom Jones, a Black clergyman in Philadelphia, shortly after the turn of the 19th century led a delegation presenting a petition to the President of the United States demanding the freedom of slaves.

One of the most articulate Christian leaders of the 19th Century was Henry Highland Garnet. Garnet and other leaders like him used the Christian religious expression and its principles to encourage Black people to stand against the forces of oppression. In an address

given to "Slaves of the United States," these thoughts were expressed:

> The bleeding captive pled his innocence, and pointed to Christianity which stood weeping at the Cross. Jehovah frowned upon the nefarious institution, and thunderbolts, red with vengeance, struggled to leap forth to blast the guilty wrtches who maintained it. But all was in vain. Slavery had stretched its dark wings of death over the land, the church stood silently by—the priests prophesied falsely, and the people love to have it so. . . .
>
> It is in your power so to torment the God-cursed slaveholders that they will let you go free. . . . Yes, the tyrants would meet with plagues more terrible than those of Pharaoh. But you are a patient people. . . . In the name of God, we ask, are you men? Where is the blood of your fathers? . . . Your dead fathers speak to you from their graves. Heaven, as with a voice of thunder, calls on you to arise from the dust.*

There is abundant documentation that many religious leaders have taken strong positions against the oppression of Black people because of their faith in Jesus Christ. This indicates that the Black man has never bought totally the white man's view of what the Christian religious expression should be. History also indicates. unfortunately, that many Black leaders did follow the biased white concept of the Christian religion.

Jesus Christ's ministry was clearly identified with the alienated and the oppressed of His society. This points up a key characteristic of the substance of the Christian religious expression. It finds its meaning and source in the life and teachings of Jesus Christ. Jesus did not depend on the status quo for sustenance

---

*Peter Williams, Jr., was the son of Peter Williams, one of the founders of the African Methodist Episcopal Zion Church in New York City. The son became an Episcopalian, was educated for the ministry and served at St. Philip's church in New York City.

  Nathaniel Paul was pastor of the African Baptist Society of Albany, New York.

†Woodson, Carter G. *The Negro Orators and Their Orations*, Washington, D.C., 1925, page 65.

*Woodson, Carter G. *The Negro Orators and Their Orations*, Washington, D.C., 1925, pp 151–152 and 157.

and identity. In fact, He attacked it. He got his support from the humanizing acts He performed for the despised and oppressed. The Christian religion, institutionalized in American society, has nurtured an oppressive white racism which is clearly not what Jesus was all about. When men like Henry H. Garnet spoke, they were the voices of Jesus.

Since the Christian religious expression has increasingly become the religion of the status quo, and since God is personified in Jesus Christ, Jesus as symbolized in white society presents a problem. White society is the oppressor of black people and it has "caucasianized" its God to fit its image. This is the white man's creation because the fact is that historically and anthropologically speaking Jesus was not a "white man." This kind of information has not been presented to the Black Christian religious community.

It is well to establish that the white Christian religious expression is status-quo oriented. The Black expression has an opportunity to be the religious arm of Black people that reflects the source of the Christian religion. Black people are the oppressed and alienated of American society. This is where the Black church and Black churchmen must stand to be representative of Jesus Christ and His teachings.

Brief Historical Perspective

There is a spirit which binds Afro-Americans in a way that we can never be bound to any other Americans because of their different histories. This spirit, a historical religious force, which united all Afro-Americans in a brotherhood which takes precedence over individual patterns for the worship of God, is rooted in racial unity for freedom and liberation.

Afro-American religion began amidst oppression and suffering in the cotton fields. Slaves were not initially permitted

families of their own, nor to protect their women from the desires of the plantation owners and their associates. But they were permitted to work out their own peculiar religion. The slave songs, which antedated the Afro-American family were used to articulate an overwhelming concern with freedom and liberation.

The genius of Ante-Bellum Afro-American religion is not readily understandable apart from an awareness of life for Afro-Americans. Black religion in America began under the camouflage of camp meetings and musical song fests which created the spirituals that provided a cover for black preachers to lead insurrections and escapes. Men such as Nat Turner were inspired by the Afro-American religious force to lead insurrections. The whole language of the underground railroad as an escape mechanism was developed through the use of spirituals as coded messages from train conductors like Harriet Tubman.

In short, the spirit of Ante-Bellum Black religion was one of revolt and liberation. Its chief exponents were men and women dedicated to the causes of freedom, liberation, and a mass exodus from slavery. The fervor of this black zeal is highly visible in the words of Rev. Henry Highland Garnet who in 1843 addressed the National Negro convention with these words:

> Brethren, arise, arise, arise! Strike for your lives and liberty. Now is the day and the hour. . . .
> Let your motto be resistance, resistance, resistance! No oppressed people have ever secured their liberty without resistance. . . .

Inspired by the hope which accompanied the end of chattel slavery, the Afro-American religious force centered in the congregation and the preacher, became a relief agency to aid the Freedman. But that hope for minister and fellowship was not realized. In this era of decline, in the quest for freedom and liberation, the minister remained the spokesman of the people with this difference: he gave in to the bribery of whites and became a traitor to his own people. Instead of freedom he preached an irrelevant personal morality and emphasized rewards in the life beyond rather than liberation from his white oppressors in much the same manner as did the white missionaries.

The songs that were once coded messages about liberation became, in fact, prevented symbols of his oppression and degradation: signs of the emerging spiritual bondage of the Afro-American religion. Thus the dominant themes of liberation and freedom were stymied in the Black religious institution and subsequently became articulated in secular society.

It was in this period of Afro-American Christianity that the emphasis on mass conversions, personal morality, and piety laid the ground work for the development of an irrelevant and misdirected religion for Blacks. It encouraged an escape into the phantasy of otherworldliness. This confusion of personal salvation and morality instead of collective liberation dealt a blow to Afro-American religion that has not been overcome to this very day.

There is, however, one positive factor in the post-reconstruction period. It was during this period that the new independent, all-Black denominations were to enjoy their greatest development and growth. These Black denominations were founded as Black institutions but were subsequently perverted into imitations of white institutions that acted as a primary force in the oppression of Black people.

Since the 1870's the Afro-American religious force of liberation has been virtually non-existant in the church. From 1920 on, the once subordinate and latent stream of white nationalism, wearing the guise of Christianity, became dominant in the Black church.

It served to keep the Black pulpit from being a forum for liberation and made it a tool to justify cowardly capitulation to white racism, which meant the oppression of Black people for the material gains of white people.

The Peril of Integration

The single most important task of Black religion is to persuade unaware Black churchmen that the much-heralded goal of integration, defined solely by whites and in terms of white interests, is not the highway to our highest hopes but a perilous journey to the continued emasculation and oppression of Black people. It is the shattering of this beloved illusion of middle class Negroes—so patently demeaning to Black pride and Black self-determination—that will ultimately determine whether or not Black religion can reverse the trend of its declining influence and recover its historic role as a liberating force in the Black community.

But dreams and illusions do not die easily, even when confronted with the harsh realities of conflicting and contradictory evidence. And it is both the harsh realities of life for Black Americans and the brutal contradictions to their coveted dreams that expose the goal of integration for what it is—the façade of a democratically inspired theory of racial unity masking a racist strategy to contain Black folk for the purpose of exploitation. While the false promises of integration always appeal, the strategy inevitably results in the psychic and material brutalization of the Black community by any means necessary, blatant or subtle, barbaric or sophisticated.

Churchmen still committed to "social justice" on integrationist terms need only weigh the "intellectual genocide" of Black students, the emasculation of the Black man in the nation's economic landscape, white America's demonic creation of ghettoes into compounds of contempt, the violence unto death by hunger of Black babies residing on white plantations in a land of unprecedented affluence, the singularly most segregated hour of eleven o'clock every Sunday morning when Christians gather for worship, and he will clearly see that this illusory promise of integration is, in very fact, the instrument of his continued oppression.

So called middle-class Black people must come to realize that they can no longer keep faith either with their Black brother or with their God in pursuit of some lofty and remote, if not irrelevant, ideal of integration while living in a land calculatingly moving toward the extinction of Black people who the whites now view as a liability. White America has never demonstrated the will or the ability to move honestly and consistently in the direction of racial reconciliation.

> "The game we [White Americans] are playing," says Lerone Bennett, Jr., "is racism. Negroes are not condemned in America because they lack education; they are condemned because they are Negroes. The truth of the matter is that neither Jesus Christ, nor Gandhi, nor Brooks Brothers, nor Yale, nor General Motors have been sufficiently persuasive in the ethic of white man to make him treat Negroes as human beings."*

Black churchmen, consciously Black and consciously Christian, in swelling

*Confrontation: Black and White, Pelican paperback, Chicago, 1965.

numbers are attesting to the bankruptcy of integration as a religious option. They call upon their Black brothers to repudiate both the symbol and the substance of the white man's integration; to disavow, in the conduct of their faith and in faithfulness to their people, the sanctity of whiteness and the beguiling illusions of brotherhood which dazzle with the rhetoric of the "brother" and destroy with the reality of the "hood." They further call upon their Black brothers to reject charity for justice, white supremacy for Black pride, white tokenism for Black self-determination, the mythology of the American dream for the truth of the Afro-American experience, white paternalism for Black power, white assimilation for Black nationalism, and civil rights for human rights—the right to be men, to be regarded and treated as human beings.

Black churchmen, in increasing numbers and on their own initiative, through newly created or long-standing instrumentalities, are opting for Black nationalism as the only viable alternative for developing an authentic religious experience for Afro-Americans.

The Promise of Black Nationalism

When one views the contemporary Black church it becomes abundantly clear that its main purposes, with one exception, do not serve the needs of the people who attend these churches; but quite the contrary, they serve the needs of the larger exploitative society. Since this is the case, the Black church can be easily indicted for having failed to meet its institutional responsibility to the Black community. The function of an institution is to organize in as effective a pattern as possible, those customs and practices of a community that aid it in its survival and stimulate it in its growth. Therefore, the function of the religious force is to organize those customs, practices and understandings that the community has embodied as its most important reality. This reality must define and clarify this particular community's reason for remaining as a group. It must strengthen the individual's reasons for living as a positive and creative part of that society. Religious force should be instrumental in enabling the people of the society to live together in trust and confidence toward and between each other. The religious institution should make it possible for the wisdom of one generation to be passed on to the next. It should embody truths and experiences that clarify the pitfalls that cause the breakdowns in human relationships. It should warn about the frailty and fright of the human heart as it inappropriately seeks to satisfy itself through greed and ignorance, thereby helping to decrease the possibility of this evil phenomenon occurring in the society in which the institution is functioning. The truth about the history concerning Black people in America is the tragic irony that institutions functioned in the Black community not for the needs of Black people but rather for the needs of white people; and the religious institution, together with other Black institutions, failed in its responsibility to develop a viable culture.

Now that the movement of Black people is clearly in the direction of forming a cohesive group, the Black church as well as other Black organizations are awakening to their task of helping to accomplish the needed unity of Black people. The Black church sees, more than ever, the awesome responsibility of helping to strengthen a people in a revolutionary situation with the moral fiber and muscle that will enable them to keep their eye on the good, as they viciously fight to rid the world of the reign of evil that has terrorized the vast majority of

human beings for the past 400 years. For a fully human society, the Black religious force has the responsibility of inculcating and sustaining an authentic morality.

It will be no simple task to build a Black religious institution, any more than it will be easy to build any institution in the Black community. The novelty of the idea of strengthening the culture that will serve our needs will demand integrity and creativity. Our tendency will be to fall back on those institutional patterns that have been controlling us ever since we can remember, and to use them as models for the kinds of institution that we feel that we will need. The Black community must be frank and honest in its tacit admission that for all intents and purposes most of the institutional patterns surrounding us will be of no use to us whatsoever, for they are built on the very principle we are fighting against. The Black religious force will, in all likelihood, be devoid of denominationalism, sectarianism and any of the kind of religious traditions that we are used to in America. Unlike the present-day Black church, it will have to be authentically Black and Afro-American. It is our position that there is no such entity presently existing in the Black community; an entity that is authentically Black. We must be cautious not to mistake thoughtless emotionalism or empty intellectualism as authentic marks of the Black church; but rather we will have to use for a model our authentic prototype that existed in the slave church. When we analyze the Afro-American religious force as it was experienced in the slave community, we discover, as we have already indicated in this paper, that it was committed to the liberation of Black people; and it embodied all of its spiritual strength toward that end. Similarly, the emerging Black religious institution must also encourage and strengthen the Black community toward this holy goal of liberation.

It is our hope that Black clergy and Black theological students continue to awaken to this task. It is our intention that Black clergy and Black theological students commit themselves to the liberation of Black people in the same manner that we have committed ourselves to the faith of Jesus Christ. We hope that our brothers and sisters in the Black community will be able to understand that in most cases our commitment is to Christ and not to Christianity. For us there must be no difficulty in viewing Christ and the other founders of the world's great religions as clearly prototypes and examples of revolutionary figures that were committed to the eradication of evil systems. Since the leader we profess to follow was unshakeably committed to this cause, it is therefore clear that we have no choice but to have the same kind of commitment.

APPENDIX G

BLACK THEOLOGY *

A Statement of the National Committee of Black Churchmen

Produced by the Committee on Theological Prospectus. Issued June 13, 1969 at Interdenominational Theological Center, Atlanta, Georgia

Why Black Theology?

Black people affirm their being. This affirmation is made in the whole experience of being black in the hostile American society. Black Theology is not a gift of the Christian gospel dispensed to slaves; rather it is an *appropriation* which black slaves made of the gospel given by their white oppressors. Black theology has been nurtured, sustained and passed on in the black churches in their various ways of expression. Black theology has dealt with all the ultimate and violent issues of life and death for a people despised and degraded.

*Additional copies can be obtained by writing: National Committee of Black Churchmen, 110 East 125th Street, New York, N.Y.

The black church has not only nurtured black people but enabled them to survive brutalities that ought not to have been inflicted on any community of men. Black theology is the product of black Christian experience and reflection. It comes out of the past. It is strong in the present. And we believe it is redemptive for the future.

This indigenous theological formation of faith emerged from the stark need of the fragmented black community to affirm itself as a part of the Kingdom of God. White theology sustained the American slave system and negated the humanity of blacks. This indigenous black theology, based on the imaginative black experience, was the best hope for the survival of black people. This is a way of saying that black theology was already present in the spirituals and slave songs and exhortations of slave preachers and their descendants.

All Theologies arise out of communal experience with God. At this moment in time, the black community seeks to express its theology in language that speaks to the contemporary mood of black people

What Is Black Theology?

Black theology is a theology of black liberation. It seeks to plumb the black condition in the light of God's revelation in Jesus Christ, so that the black community can see that the gospel is commensurate with the achievement of black humanity. Black Theology is a theology of "blackness." It is the affirmation of black humanity that emancipates black people from white racism thus providing authentic freedom for both white and black people. It affirms the humanity of white people in that it says No to the encroachment of white oppression.

The message of liberation is the revelation of God as revealed in the incarnation of Jesus Christ. Freedom *is* the gospel. Jesus is the Liberator! "He . . . hath sent me to preach deliverance to the captives." (Luke 4:18) Thus the black patriarchs and we ourselves know this reality despite all attempts of the white church to obscure it and to utilize Christianity as a means of enslaving blacks. The demand that Christ the Liberator imposes on all men *requires* all blacks to affirm their full dignity as persons and all whites to surrender their presumptions of superiority and abuses of power.

What Does This Mean?

It means that Black Theology must confront the issues which are a part of the reality of black oppression. We cannot ignore the powerlessness of the black community. Despite the *repeated*

requests for significant programs of social change, the American people have refused to appropriate adequate sums of money for social reconstruction. White church bodies have often made promises only to follow with default. We must, therefore, once again call the attention of the nation and the church to the need for providing adequate sources of power (reparation).

Reparation is a part of the Gospel message. Zacchaeus knew well the necessity for repayment as an essential ingredient in repentance. "If I have taken anything from any man by false accusation, I restore him fourfold." (Luke 19:8) The church which calls itself the servant church must, like its Lord, be willing to strip itself of possessions in order to build and restore that which has been destroyed by the compromising bureaucrats and conscienceless rich. While reparation cannot remove the guilt created by the despicable dead of slavery, it is nonetheless, a positive response to the need for power in the black community. This nation, and, a people who have always related the value of the person to his possession of property, must recognize the necessity of restoring property in order to reconstitute personhood.

What Is the Cost?

Living is risk. We take it in confidence. The black community has been brutalized and victimized over the centuries. The recognition that comes from seeing Jesus as Liberator and the Gospel as freedom empowers black men to risk themselves for freedom and for faith. This faith we affirm in the midst of a hostile, disbelieving society. We intend to exist by this faith at all times and in all places.

In spite of brutal deprivation and denial the black community has appropriated the spurious form of Christianity imposed upon it and made it into an instrument for resisting the extreme demands of oppression. It has enabled the black community to live through unfulfilled promises, unnecessary risks, and inhuman relationships.

As black theologians address themselves to the issues of the black revolution, it is incumbent upon them to say that the black community will not be turned from its course, but will seek complete fulfillment of the promises of the Gospel. Black

people have survived the terror. We now commit ourselves to the risks of affirming the dignity of black personhood. We do this as men and as black Christians. This is the message of Black theology. In the words of Eldredge Cleaver,

We shall have our manhood.
We shall have it or the earth will be
    leveled by our efforts to gain it.

APPENDIX H

EXPANDED STATEMENT OF LONG RANGE GOALS

Adopted in Convention, June 1969
Union of Black Clergy and Laity of the Episcopal Church

1. We affirm that our struggle to survive and be free in this society and in this church is a continuation of an on-going history. We salute the brave men and women of the past, who in the ways that time and temper would allow, labored to bring before the Church its mission of reconciliation and its commitment to Christ. The Church, however, has responded with indifference, tokenism and subterfuge. Therefore, we pledge our time, talents and resources to the eradication of racism in the Episcopal Church— if indeed that body is redeemable.

2. That we undertake our internal obligation as a union the protecting and ministering to the needs of each other as brothers. We recognize that mission status in the Episcopal Church is a plantation system in which the poor and non-white are relegated to the politics of dependency and non-power. By this

archaic system monotonously the church profits from and contributes to (both by hard cash and moral justification) the exploitation of masses of people and also serves as an obstacle to the liberation of non-whites.

We therefore see our role as that of establishing the equality and humanity of every child of God, removing the shackles of malevolent welfare and financial insecurity from both clergy and lay Episcopalians.

3. We affirm our solidarity with the absolute goal of self-determination of the black community both inside and outside the church. We assert that our highest priority is the survival of black people. We see the black movement as the movement of the Holy Spirit in this nation and in the world. We call upon each

national, diocesan, and parish body to make such sacrifices as will assure the just and good society in which all brethren can dwell in peace.

4. We finally affirm that this Union shall be a community where brothers will speak honestly, patiently, and in trust and in love with each other. That such dealings shall be in confidence, and only authorized spokesmen, on authorized topics, shall carry to the public what is in our interest to carry. What we speak to here is the vital goal of a new relationship of black to black with the aim of building such a sense of responsibility toward each other and to all others, that our corporate determination and commitment will be unchallenged.

APPENDIX I

A MESSAGE TO THE CHURCHES FROM OAKLAND

Third Annual Convocation, National Committee of Black Churchmen
November 11–14, 1969, Oakland, California

We came to Oakland as an act of faith. We came seeking a deeper experience of the mission of God in the contemporary world than has ever been provided by the denominations and local congregations to which some of us belong, from which some of us have fled in profound disillusionment, and which some of us have observed, but only with doubt and distrust.

In a time of the increasing institutionalization and bureaucratization of the Church we do not come to create a new institutional form of the Church. We are not here to invent a new denomination. Our primary and overreaching concern is to seek, through our common experience and consciousness of being black and powerless in a part of the world dominated by white racism and white power, a new religio-cultural, political and economic vocation which can relate to our own deep alienation from a religious, cultural, political and economic system which is not compatible with our own instincts and sensibilities but which has been commended to us and imposed upon us by white, bourgeois, European and American religious, political and economic institutions interlocking and conspiring with one another to whitenize and subordinate black people.

This new vocation to which we are called is *political* in the sense that it seeks radically to change, by whatever means are necessary, the racist structures which dominate our lives; *cultural* in the sense that it seeks to identify, recreate, unify and authenticate whatever traditions, values and styles of life are indigenous or distinctive to the black community; and *theological* in the sense that we believe that it is God—however He chooses to reveal Himself today to oppressed peoples in America and in the Third World—who has chosen black humanity as a vanguard to resist the demonic powers of racism, capitalism and imperialism, and to so reform the structures of this world that they will more perfectly minister to the peace and power of all people as children of One God and brothers of one another.

We black people are a religious people. From the earliest recorded time we have acknowledged a Supreme Being. With the fullness of our physical bodies and emotions we have unabashedly worshipped Him with shouts of joy and in the tears of pain and anguish. We neither believe that God is dead, white, nor captive to some highly rationalistic and dogmatic formulations of the Christian faith which relate him exclusively to the canons of the Old and New Testaments and accommodate Him to the reigning spirits of a socio-technical age. Rather, we affirm that God is Liberator in the man Jesus Christ, that His message is Freedom, and that today He calls all men to be what they are in themselves, and among their own people, in the context of a pluralistic world-society of dignity and self-determination for all. We believe that in a special way God's favor rests today upon the poor and oppressed peoples of the world and that He calls them to be the ministering angels of His judgment and grace as His Kingdom of Freedom and Peace breaks in from the future upon a world shackled to ancient sins and virtues and upon the present inequalities, imperialistic wars, and ambitions of privileged nations, classes and power-groups.

This call of God which we in the NCBC hear in what we have been saying to one another in Oakland is a call to suffering and sacrifice. It is a call to identification with frustrated, emasculated, downtrodden men, women and children, most of them black, to share their anguish and their hope and to work for their enlightenment and empowerment, not that they might in turn become oppressors, but that through them the world might be saved from the selfishness, greed and subjuga-

tion which has characterized the centuries-old hegemony of the white, Anglo-Saxon, European civilizations of the West.

We therefore call upon the white, Christian churches of America and Europe, which have nurtured and sustained the systems of injustice that have driven the world to the present crisis, to submit themselves to radical reformation. We challenge them to psychologically and institutionally disengage themselves from the nations within whose boundaries they have so often baptized and sanctified racism, imperialism and economic selfishness, and to take upon themselves the kind of revolutionary posture that can force the transfer of requisite countervailing power to oppressed peoples wherever they may be found. We challenge them to divest themselves of their own great wealth—much of it ill-gotten—built upon the bodies of exploited races and classes wherever imperialistic political and economic influences have extended within and beyond national boundaries, and to make massive ecclesiastical resources of capital and technical assistance available to powerless people in Africa, Asia, Latin America and the United States.

We believe that the Black Manifesto, which was issued this year to the churches of America and to several official church convocations in Europe by the Black Economic Development Conference, is a most significant and essentially accurate assessment of the guilt and reparational responsibility of white Christendom and the wealthy Jewish communions of the United States. We reaffirm our support of that document and particularly of its programmatic objectives with respect to the situation of black people in the United States, Africa and the Caribbean area.

The NCBC will not desist from calling the white religious establishment of the United States to the full and immediate implementation of the demands of the Manifesto. Nor will we excuse from participation in the achievement of its objectives the historic black churches of America which have left undone many of the things they ought to have done in the slums and rural ghettoes of the United States, Africa and the West Indes.

We do not shrink from the revolutionary, anti-capitalistic implications of the Manifesto. While all of our members do not give unqualified endorsement to every strategy and tactic stated or implied in the original document issued in Detroit, the National Committee of Black Churchmen, as a body, is committed to the essential spirit and meaning of the analysis and proposals, and will continue to press them upon the churches and . synagogues of America, upon the National Council of Churches in the U.S.A., and upon the World Council of Churches.

We demand that individual white church agencies and white brethren, who call themselves our allies, recognize the imperative nature and urgency of this task in light of the crisis that is upon us in the cities and depressed rural areas in this most affluent and powerful nation of the world.

By the faith of our fathers, by the faith of Nat Turner and Denmark Vesey, of Allen and Varick , of Delany, of Garvey and DuBois and Martin Luther King, Jr., and Malcolm X, and by the grace of God, the NCBC has undertaken in cooperation with IFCO and BEDC,* to call this nation, beginning with the white churches, which have a clear and acknowledged

*Interreligious Foundation for Community Organization, Inc., and the Black Economic Development Conference.—Ed.

moral responsibility, to the conference table to negotiate in good faith the transfer of power to those segments of society which have been deprived of freedom, justice and self-determination. It *can* be done. It can be done peacefully. *It must be done* in any case, or peace, brotherhood and reconciliation will remain empty, mocking words in an American wasteland of racial hatred and strife. Now is the time to act, for as the words of Isaiah 42 sternly remind us in every nation and generation: "He will not rest nor be silent until He has established justice in the earth. . . ."

Having thus analyzed our situation, and being ready and determined to respond to the promptings of this same God, we have been made to recognize that it is not enough simply to call the white churches to the negotiation table. Long, agonizing months of fruitless negotiations with these churches, in efforts to lead them to recognize and to fund the Black Economic Development Conference, have forced us sadly to acknowledge the harsh reality that the white churches and church structures are not capable of positive responses to the considered opinions of their black peers. We accept the defiance of us which this exposes; but we intend to do several things about that defiance. We are unalterably committed to the effecting of a more equitable power balance "by whatever means are necessary." Means additional to negotiation are now necessary. The time has come for us to resort to the use of unusual forms of pressure upon the white church structures if we are ever to realize the legitimate goal of a literal transferral of power.

One of the chief symbols of white church power is the institution known as the National Council of Churches of Christ in the U.S.A. That institution—not unlike the World Council of Churches, the myriad regional and local councils of churches, and the white denominations themselves—is a sorry example of institutionalized white decision-making power. This is true notwithstanding the fact that it has token representation of blacks in executive capacity. The General Secretary is white; the Deputy General Secretary is white; all of the Associate General Secretaries are white; the heads of divisions which are of critical relevance to the black condition, such as the Division of Christian Life and Mission, the Division of Overseas Ministries, and the Division of Christian Education are white. These are untenable and thoroughly unacceptable realities. They comprise an affront to black churchmen everywhere.

We, therefore, announce our dedication to a battle which must culminate in the appointment of a black General Secretary of the N.C.C., and in the designation of black churchmen, in significant numbers, at the level of Associate General Secretaries and division heads. These appointments must be black churchmen who come not only from the ranks of the white denominations, but who presently labor within the fold of the great, historical black communions. The day has passed when we can be played one against the other. The NCBC, therefore, in concert with black churchmen everywhere, will determine whom you shall appoint.

Time and circumstance have met in such a way as to place us, at this day, on the virtual eve of the convening of the General Assembly of the National Council of Churches. That assembly will meet in the city of Detroit during the first week of December, 1969. In the light of our deliberations in Oakland, and in view of the stance which we have been forced by white recalcitrance to take, we declare our intention to assure that that General

Assembly is confronted with the serious issues which here we have raised. One way or another, that General Assembly shall deal with this aspect of the Black agenda. We have neither the need nor the intention to divulge the means by which we shall accomplish this end. We simply announce that sufficient pressures shall be brought to bear upon the Assembly to cause it to deal with these issues. Whether it deals wisely or foolishly with them is for the Assembly to determine. We are persuaded that mere suggestions and reasonable arguments are lost in the mires of verbiage and referrals which are so readily spawned by white church institutions. To us, "black empowerment" means, precisely, black empowerment; it does not mean endless dialogue with persons and institutions which have demonstrated a propensity for eternal, infernal dialogue.

When the N.C.C., in 1967, spoke of a "Crisis in the Nation," it was speaking of the black condition. It named that Crisis as one of the two top priorities for programming and funding. Yet, as the N.C.C., and as every black churchman knows, little enough has been done by that institution literally to re-order its priorities in line with its eloquent statement. We are convinced that only the transfer of power, at significant levels, can help to bring progress in this area of alleged concern. Detroit must see the establishment of our efforts to accomplish this goal. The battle once begun, we pledge ourselves to the vigorous pursuit of these objectives, by whatever means are necessary, until victory is won. If it should be that racism and white negativism are, indeed, so vital a part of the reality of the N.C.C. that it would choose to destroy itself before acceding to these just insistences, then it is clear that the N.C.C. is incapable of becoming relevant to blacks, and being thus irrelevant, would serve a more Christian purpose in its demise than it would in a continuation of its present disguise.

Let no white churches, church institutions or churchmen seek comfort in the fact that we place our present focus upon the National Council of Churches.

It is only the accidental timing of the meeting of the General Assembly which directs us so to do. Let the World Council of Churches know, assuredly, that it is programmed into our agenda; let every regional and local council of churches across this land know, without doubt, that our intentions and our agenda speak to them all; let all national and regional denominations, judicatories, dioceses and what-have-you know that this day we are speaking to them in tones of clarion sound. Our agenda for the white church structures is all-embracing. Fidelity to Jesus Christ, the Lord of all, informs us that none may be allowed the deceptive comfort of respite.

Our deliberations in Oakland have led us to know that it was for the clarification of these purposes that we were brought to Oakland, and it is with these resolutions and determinations that, under God's guidance, we return to our individual places and ramparts to work, to strive, and to fight.

Let all of the church of God say, "Amen!"

APPENDIX J

BLACK DECLARATION OF INDEPENDENCE

an Advertisement Which Appeared in The New York Times
Friday, July 3, 1970

IN THE BLACK COMMUNITY, July 4, 1970 A DECLARATION by concerned Black Citizens of the United States of America in Black Churches, Schools, Homes, Community Organizations and Institutions assembled:

When in the course of Human Events, it becomes necessary for a People who were stolen from the lands of their Fathers, transported under the most ruthless and brutal circumstances 5,000 miles to a strange land, sold into dehumanizing slavery, emasculated, subjugated, exploited and discriminated against for 351 years, to call, with finality, a halt to such indignities and genocidal practices—by virtue of the Laws of Nature and of Nature's God, a decent respect to the Opinions of Mankind requires that they should declare their just grievances and the urgent and necessary redress thereof.

We hold these truths to be self-evident, that all Men are not *only* created equal and endowed by their Creator with certain unalienable rights among which are Life, Liberty and the Pursuit of Happiness, but that when this equality and these rights are deliberately and consistently refused, withheld or abnegated, men are bound by self-respect and honor to rise up in righteous indignation to secure them. Whenever any Form of Government, or any variety of established traditions and systems of the Majority becomes destructive of Freedom and of legitimate Human Rights, it is the Right of the Minorities to use every necessary and accessible means to protest and to disrupt the machinery of

Oppression, and so to bring such general distress and discomfort upon the oppressor as to the offended Minorities shall seem most appropriate and most likely to effect a proper adjustment of the society.

Prudence, indeed, will dictate that such bold tactics should not be initiated for light and transient Causes; and, accordingly, the Experience of White America has been that the descendants of the African citizens brought forcibly to these shores, and to the shores of the Caribbean Islands, as slaves, have been patient long past what can be expected of any human beings so affronted. But when a long train of Abuses and Violence, pursuing invariably the same Object, manifests a Design to reduce them under Absolute Racist Domination and Injustice, it is their Duty radically to confront such Government or system of traditions, and to provide, under the aegis of Legitimate Minority Power and Self Determination, for their present Relief and future Security. Such has been the patient Sufferance of Black People in the United States of America; and such is now the Necessity which constrains them to address this Declaration to Despotic White Power, and to give due notice of their determined refusal to be any longer silenced by fear or flattery, or to be denied justice. The history of the treatment of Black People in the United States is a history having in direct Object the Establishment and Maintenance of Racist Tyranny over this People. To prove this, let Facts be submitted to a candid World.

The United States has evaded Compliance to laws the most wholesome and necessary for our Children's education.

The United States has caused us to be isolated in the most dilapidated and unhealthful sections of all cities.

The United States has allowed election districts to be so gerrymandered that Black People find the right to Representation in the Legislatures almost impossible of attainment.

The United States has allowed the dissolution of school districts controlled by Blacks when Blacks opposed with manly Firmness the white man's Invasions on the Rights of our People.

The United States has erected a Multitude of Public Agencies and Offices, and sent into our ghettos Swarms of Social Workers, Officers and Investigators to harass our People, and eat out their Substance to feed the Bureaucracies.

The United States has kept in our ghettos, in Times of Peace, Standing Armies of Police, State Troopers and National Guardsmen, without the consent of our People.

The United States has imposed Taxes upon us without protecting our Constitutional Rights.

The United States has constrained our Black sons taken Captive in its Armies to bear arms against their black, brown and yellow Brothers, to be the Executioners of these Friends and Brethren, or to fall themselves by their Hands.

The Exploitation and Injustice of the United States have incited domestic Insurrections among us, and the United States has endeavored to bring on the Inhabitants of our ghettos, the merciless Military Establishment, whose known Rule of control is an undistinguished shooting of all Ages, Sexes, and Conditions of Black People:

For being lynched, burned, tortured, harried, harassed and imprisoned without Just Cause.

For being gunned down in the streets, in our churches, in our homes, in our apartments and on our campuses, by Policemen and Troops who are protected by a Mock Trial, from Punishment for any Murders which they commit on the Inhabitants of our Communities.

For creating, through Racism and bigotry, an unrelenting Economic Depression in the Black Community which wreaks havoc upon our men and disheartens our youth.

For denying to most of us equal access to the better Housing and Education of the land.

For having desecrated and torn down our humblest dwelling places, under the Pretense of Urban Renewal, without replacing them at costs we can afford.

The United States has denied our personhood by refusing to teach our heritage, and the magnificent contributions to the life, wealth and growth of this Nation which have been made by Black People.

In every stage of these Oppressions we have Petitioned for Redress in the most humble terms: Our repeated Petitions have been answered mainly by repeated Injury. A Nation, whose Character is thus marked by every act which may define a Racially Oppressive Regime, is unfit to receive the respect of a Free People.

Nor have we been wanting in attentions to our White Brethren. We have warned them from time to time of Attempts by their Structures of Power to extend an unwarranted, Repressive Control over us. We have reminded them of the Circumstances of our Captivity and Settlement here. We have appealed to their vaunted Justice and Magnanimity, and we have conjured them by the Ties of our Common Humanity to disavow these Injustices, which would inevitably interrupt our Connections and Correspondence. They have been deaf to the voice of Justice and of Humanity. We must, therefore, acquiesce in the Necessity, which hereby announces our Most Firm Commitment to the Liberation of Black People, and hold the Institutions, Traditions and Systems of the United States as we hold the rest of the societies of Mankind, Enemies when Unjust and Tyrannical; when Just and Free, Friends.

We, therefore, the Black People of the United States of America, in all parts of this Nation, appealing to the Supreme Judge of the World for the Rectitude of our Intentions, do, in the Name of our good People and our own Black Heroes— Richard Allen, James Varick, Absalom Jones, Nat Turner, Frederick Douglass, Marcus Garvey, Malcolm X, Martin Luther King, Jr., and all Black People past and present, great and small—Solemnly Publish and Declare, that we shall be, and of Right ought to be FREE AND INDEPENDENT FROM THE INJUSTICE, EXPLOITATIVE CONTROL, INSTITUTIONALIZED VIOLENCE AND RACISM OF WHITE AMERICA, that unless we receive full Redress and Relief from these Inhumanities we will move to renounce all Allegiance to this Nation, and will refuse, in every way, to cooperate with the Evil which is Perpetrated upon ourselves and our Communities. And for the support of this Declaration, with a firm Reliance on the Protection of divine Providence, we mutually pledge to each other our Lives, our Fortunes, and our sacred Honor.

Signed, by Order and in behalf of Black People,

NATIONAL COMMITTEE OF BLACK CHURCHMEN, INC.

110 East 125th Street

New York, N.Y. 10035

Signatories and Sponsors:

*Father Lawrence Lucas, Roman Catholic, New York, New York

*Bishop H. B. Shaw. A.M.E.Z. Church, Pres. NCBC—Wilmington, North Carolina

*The Rev. Leon W. Watts, II, Associate Executive, NCBC, Brooklyn, N.Y.

*The Rev. M. L. Wilson, Convent Avenue Baptist Church, N.Y.C.

The Rev. J. Metz Rollins Jr., Executive NCBC, White Plains, New York

The Rev. Charles S. Spivey, Jr., Director Dept. Social Justice N.C.C., N.Y.C.

*The Rev. Edler G. Hawkins, St. Augustine Presbyterian Church, N.Y.C.

The Rev. Albert Cleage, Shrine of Black Madonna, Detroit, Michigan

*The Rev. Tollie Caution, Episcopal Church, New York City

The Rev. Caroll Felton, A.M.E. Zion, Chicago, Illinois

*The Rev. Will Herzfeld, Missouri-Synod Lutheran Church, Oakland, California

The Rev. Oscar McCloud, Division Church and Race, United Presbyterian

The Rev. Robert C. Chapman, Dept. Social Justice, N.C.C.

The Rev. Mance C. Jackson, C.M.E. Church, Atlanta, Georgia

The Rev. Charles J. Sargent, Jr., American Baptist Convention, N.Y.C.

*The Rev. Gilbert H. Caldwell, Executive Ministerial Interfaith Assoc., N.Y.C.

The Rev. John P. Collier, A.M.E. Church, New York, New York

*The Rev. Calvin B. Marshall, III, Varick Memorial A.M.E.Z. Church, Brooklyn, N.Y.

The Rev. Quinland Gordon, Episcopal Church, New York, New York

The Rev. James E. Jones, Westminster Presbyterian Church, Los Angeles, Calif.

The Rev. John H. Adams, Grant A.M.E. Church, Los Angeles, Calif.

Mr. Hayward Henry, Black Unitarian-Universalists Caucus, Boston, Massachusetts

The Rev. Vaughn T. Eason, A.M.E.Z. Church, Philadelphia, Pennsylvania

The Rev. R. L. Speaks, First A.M.E.Z. Church, Brooklyn, New York

The Rev. Charles L. Warren, Executive, Council of Churches of Greater Washington, D.C.

The Rev. E. Wellington Butts, II, National Chairman, Black Presbyterians United, Englewood, New Jersey

The Rev. Jefferson P. Rogers, Church of the Redeemer, Presbyterian, U.S. Washington, D.C.

Miss Janet Douglas, New York, New York

Mrs. Frank E. Jones, New York, New York

The Rev. Lawrence A. Miller, A.M.E.Z. Church, Durham, North Carolina

The Rev. Bennie Whiten, New York City Mission Society, New York, N.Y.

The Rev. George McMurray, A.M.E.Z., New York, New York

The Rev. Charles Cobb, U.C.C. Commission on Racial Justice, New York, N.Y.

*The Rev. William C. Ardrey, A.M.E.Z., Detroit, Michigan

The Rev. Clarence Cave, United Presbyterian Church, Philadelphia, Pennsylvania

The Rev. J. Clinton Hoggard, A.M.E.Z. Church, New York, New York

Black Economic Development Conference, Brooklyn, New York

I.F.C.O. Black Caucus, New York, New York

The Ministerial Interfaith Association, New York, New York

The Rev. W. Marcus Williams, Antioch Baptist Church North, Atlanta, Georgia 30318

The Rev. James M. Lawson, United Methodist Church, Memphis, Tenn.

*Members of Executive Committee

BIBLIOGRAPHY

of References and Books for Further Reading

Aptheker, Herbert 1969 *American Negro Slave Revolts.* New York: International Publishers Co.

Berton, Pierre 1965 *The Comfortable Pew.* Philadelphia, Lippincott

Cleage, Albert 1969 *The Black Messiah.* New York: Sheed & Ward

Cone, James H
 1969 *Black Theology and Black Power.* New York: Seabury
 1970 *A Black Theology of Liberation.* Philadelphia, Pa: Lippincott
 1972 *The Spirituals and the Blues.* New York: Seabury

Davidson, Basil 1959 *The Lost Cities of Africa.* Boston, Mass: Little, Brown

Fanon, Franz 1968 *The Wretched of the Earth.* New York: Grove

Franklin, John Hope 1967 *From Slavery to Freedom.* New York: Knopf

Frazier, E Franklin 1963 *The Negro Church in America.* New York: Schocken

Garnet, Henry Highland 1969 *An Address to the Slaves of the United States of America.* New York: Arno Press

Grier, William, and Cobbs, Price M 1968 *Black Rage.* New York: Basic Books

Gutierrez, Gustavo 1973 *A Theology of Liberation.* New York: Orbis

Jones, Major J 1971 *Black Awareness: A Theology of Hope.* Nashville, Tennesee: Abingdon

Jones, William 1973 *Is God a White Racist? Preamble to Black Theology.* New York: Doubleday

Lovell, John, Jr 1972 *Black Song: The Forge and the Flame.* New York: Macmillan

Mays, Benjamin E 1969 *The Negro God: As Reflected in His Literature.* New York: Atheneum

Roberts, J Deotis 1971 *Liberation and Reconciliation: A Black Theology.* Philadelphia, Pa: Westminster

Thurman, Howard 1949 *Jesus and the Disinherited.* Nashville, Tennessee: Abingdon

Walker, David 1969 *Walker's Appeal in Four Articles* New York: Arno Press

Washington, Joseph R
 1964 *Black Religion: The Negro and Christianity in the United States.* Boston, Massachusetts: Beacon
 1969 *The Politics of God.* Boston, Massachusetts: Beacon

Wilmore, Gayraud S 1972 *Black Religion and Black Radicalism.* New York: Doubleday

Woodson, Carter G 1945 *The History of the Negro Church.* Washington, D.C.: Associated Publishers

Woodward, C Vann 1966 *The Strange Career of Jim Crow.* New York: Oxford University Press